OCT 4 '77	JUL 1 2 1990	
AUG 18 '78	JUL 1 3 1990	
OCT 29 '78		
NOV 20 '79		
APR 1 7 '80		
MAY 7 '80		
MAY 7 '80		
MAR 1 1983		

Tennis
Psychology

Tennis Psychology

Harold Geist, Ph.D.
Lecturer, Department of Psychology
San Francisco State University

and

Cecilia A. Martinez
Touring Professional
Virginia Slims—USTA
Women's Professional Tour

Nelson-Hall nh Chicago

LIBRARY OF CONGRESS CATALOGING IN PUBLICATION DATA

Geist, Harold.
  Tennis psychology.

  Includes index.
    1. Tennis—Psychological aspects. I. Martinez,
Cecilia A., joint author. II. Title.
GV1002.9.P75G44   796.34'201   75-17651
ISBN 0-88229-120-3

to Margaret

Contents

Foreword

In my career as a tennis player around the world, I have found that in addition to technique, psychology has played an extremely important part in my winning game. In the following pages the authors have lucidly related elements of the psychological aspects of tennis that readers will be able to use to improve their own game. In addition, the public will get a glimpse of life on the professional tennis circuit, which, I hope will enhance appreciation of top competitive tennis. I hope everyone will read this book with interest and profit.

ROSEMARY CASALS

Acknowledgments

The authors would like to thank many people who made this book possible. First, Russel Freeman and Robert Benjamin, who suggested what to include and not to include. Then Catherine Martinez, mother of the female author and a tennis player in her own right, who gave us suggestions and moral support throughout the writing of the manuscript. Finally, to the typists who labored over the manuscript—Anita Andrews, Julie Kaplow, and Peggi Oakley—we are also grateful.

chapter one

About the Game

Interest in tennis has grown very rapidly in recent years because the general public finds it relatively inexpensive and convenient to play. The game is tremendously popular with men, women, and children of all ages. It is estimated that about 25 million people play tennis today and that over 50 million people watched the Billie Jean King–Bobby Riggs match.

To play, all you need is a minimum of equipment (at minimal cost), a court, and one other person. In contrast to golf, another sport enjoyed by great numbers of people, tennis has the advantage of requiring less expensive and cumbersome equipment. In addition, tennis courts are often more accessible than golf courses and more of them are likely to exist in any given area.

Tennis is excellent exercise (if you don't keep the ball in play, you'll be chasing it over a wide area). It is a good family sport (youngsters can play, and women can compete against men). It is a social sport and a business sport, too— an informal way to meet people or business contacts, particularly in friendly mixed doubles. In addition, tennis provides a way to release tensions and aggression as you take out frustrations on the ball and your opponent. When played at an advanced level, tennis also can be a reflection of creative expression and supreme grace.

Tennis has a long history and was first played in the United States in the latter part of the nineteenth century. Lawn tennis, the predecessor of tennis, was one of various ball games that originated in Egypt and Persia around 500 B.C. Lawn tennis had its modern beginnings in England, and the name, especially in the United States, has been contracted to *tennis*.

The originator of modern lawn tennis was an Englishman, Walter Wingfield, who in 1874 devised and patented a new, hourglass-shaped portable court for playing the game. At about this time the All England Cricket Club at Wimbledon, a suburb of London, added Lawn Tennis to its name and several grass courts to its facilities. The first of all championships was held on these courts in June 1877. The English Lawn Tennis Association was founded in 1886, the International Tennis Federation in 1912. Meanwhile, the game had spread to other continents.

Lawn tennis was introduced in the United States by Mary E. Outerbridge, who spent the winter of 1874 in Bermuda and saw the game played by the British Officers of the Garrison. She returned to the States with a net, racket, and balls, and, with the help of her brother, A. Emilius Outerbridge, laid out a court on the grounds of the Staten Island Cricket and Baseball Club. Dr. James Dwight of Boston soon thereafter laid out a court at Nahaut, a seaside resort in Boston harbor. The first tournament in the United States was played at Nahaut in August 1876. The first official championships in the United States, played under English rules, were held at the Casino, Newport,

Rhode Island, on August 31, 1881. The same year, the United States Lawn Tennis Association was formed.

For many years tennis was played primarily on the eastern seaboard, but gradually the game spread across the country and came of age.

The fundamentals of tennis are quite easy to learn, but true expertise comes only with intensive practice and dedication. Significantly, tennis is a game in which the biggest and strongest players do not always prevail—a game of strategy, skill, and psychology. The boy who could not make the basketball team because he was too short, or the football team because he was too small, will find tennis very much to his liking. It is an equalizer in which skill and strategy count for more than size and strength.

Tennis is a sport for the "beautiful people" such as movie stars, socialites, senators, congressmen, even royalty. It is a sport for the average and underprivileged as well. For example, Arthur Ashe, the great black tennis star, conducts tennis clinics at playgrounds in disadvantaged neighborhoods for the Pepsi-Cola Company. The National Junior Tennis League has been created to provide instruction for youngsters. The Virginia Slims Women's Professional Group gives clinics in the cities in which they compete.

Psychology in Tennis

The psychological importance of tennis is demonstrated by the existence of various seminars, institutes, and workshops devoted to the psychology of sports, some specifically to tennis psychology. The Esalen Sports Center in San Francisco is part of the Esalen Institute devoted to the development of human potential. The Sports Center was created to discover new areas of athletic culture. Esalen's Dyveka Spino, an accomplished tennis player, dancer,

and concert pianist, has conducted tennis workshops that
focus on the psychological aspects of the game. She believes that tennis players are naturally aggressive and ener-
getic, that they love quick give-and-take and fast decisions. Victory to a tennis player is a "joyous experience";
defeat is regarded as failure. Ms. Spino believes that tennis
players ignore the importance of *total* conditioning—the
combination of such practices as weight-lifting, roadwork,
breathing exercises, and meditation. Instead of going out
and hitting thousands of balls, she says, a tennis player
should "get his total ship in shape," including his psyche.
Her thesis is that as a player masters himself, he will win
more. She believes that the Esalen Institute, and more particularly the tennis workshops, enable tennis players to
let go and "soar with the sport." Her "tennis flow" weekends
emphasize not only tennis but also relaxation, breathing
exercises, meditation, and stretching routines.

Vic Braden, the Southern California tennis coach-
psychologist, director of Braden's Tennis College at Lake
Tahoe in the summer and at Palm Springs in the winter,
has established a year-round, nonprofit research center at
Coto de Caza near Laguna Beach, California. There, re-
searchers study the psychological aspects of playing tennis.
Experiments are designed to determine the psychological
characteristics of tennis winners and losers and to study
such medico-psychological aspects as whether or not tennis
is really good exercise. Braden is also investigating the best
age to start playing the game.

In an article by Bill Bruns, "How to Beat Yourself at
Tennis,"* Braden delineates the various types of players:

    1) The unbelievable dresser. "They've got every-
    thing — sweatbands, headband, '40-love' underwear,
    embroidered tennis rackets on the towel they care-

* © 1973 *Human Behavior* Magazine. Reprinted by Permission.

fully lay over the net. But I've seldom seen really immaculate dressers, the ones with all the latest clothes, ever win a match. They place too much faith in a new pair of shorts."

2) The equipment freak. "Show me a guy with a leather case and four matching rackets—unless he's on the tour—and I'll show you a loser. Because he's probably a guy who misses his shots, loses the match and immediately runs down to the sporting goods store and buys another racket. He'll tell me crazy things like, 'This racket; I've tried it, but it has no backhands in it at all.' "

3) The trophy seeker. "He's beautiful. He looks all over the doggone country for tournaments where he might win a trophy. His needs are so great that he'll lie to get into an event, claiming he's a C player when he's really a B. I've known people who, if they don't have a good year winning trophies, will literally stage their own tournaments, buy the trophies themselves and end up winning a trophy. That's not uncommon."

4) The "sensual kind of player" with the showboat moves. "These people have developed unbelievable extra movements in their serve, and they give you all this body motion until they actually hit the ball. Then they stop and go—doink!—and hit a patty-cake shot."

5) The manipulator. "Warming up before the match he'll tell his opponent, 'I really shouldn't be playing you, I'm so much better.' Then, when he plays, he goes for speed and power, trying to overwhelm the person. But his needs seem to go beyond winning. He usually beats his opponent to the clubhouse, beats him giving the scores and beats him to telling the story as

to who won and who lost. He's the kind of person who really cannot be in a position where he feels as though he's going to be manipulated, so he must begin to manipulate immediately. This is where you have your big trouble in private clubs, because nearly everybody who belongs is a manipulator, from one standpoint or another. Most are executives in major firms and they're not used to being manipulated—and now they run up against other people who manipulate, too. The poor club manager. If he has 450 members, he has 450 people who know, in their minds, they could be doing a better job of running the facility than the manager."

6) The player who is always calling up defense mechanisms. " 'Why does the sun only shine on my side?' 'The wind is always blowing in my face.' Every time he misses a shot he checks his racket. It's an amazing thing because, as I tell my classes, the ball is round—it goes right where you hit it. So it's not your racket, it's you. Another thing, tennis is a stress situation. You're playing almost naked, you're all alone and it's very hard to find defense mechanisms that work around intelligent people. When you start saying before a match, 'Gee, I haven't played in about six months,' people see that from a mile away."

7) The male chauvinist in mixed doubles. "The man who sort of delights in playing against women. Tennis is one of the only sports where men and women can compete against each other. Very often the man is working out a lot of subconscious hostilities, especially in intermediate tennis, where he's trying to physically hurt the woman. However, a woman who can play the net well is much more valuable than the man, because the woman in mixed doubles gets 85

percent of the shots. If she can volley (return the shots), she's sensational. But most men don't see it that way. Just before the first serve, the man will say, 'Darling, big match today, right? Now, you're so valuable that I'm going to put you here'—Braden indicates a position at the extreme end of the net, nearly off the court—'and I want you to just hold the racket right in front of your face.' Well, what he is saying is, 'Look, I can play these guys alone. If I could put you on the bench I would, but it wouldn't look too good.' "

8) Another aspect of the male-female conflicts on the courts, also tied up with male virility, comes in singles— "and the ultimate humiliation, when the wife is better than the husband. There's just constant stress. The husband just won't give up. I see this happen and I say to myself, 'Why does that man keep playing his wife?' She beats his brains out. He seethes on the inside. Why can't he just say, 'Darling, you're better than me,' and then go out and play some people on his level? But he can't. He plays her all the time and it's almost a masochistic kind of thing."

A unique method of arousing interest in tennis in talented young artists is demonstrated by the fascinating program of Jack McCorkle, a fifth-grade teacher at Micheltorena School in the Silverlake area of Los Angeles, California. In addition to his teaching duties, McCorkle is a ranked senior tennis player in Southern California. Eight years ago he organized an art class of gifted youngsters from kindergarten through sixth grade. Initially, the program included only three children, but it now has grown to thirty. Currently called the Young Masters, these youngsters have sold over four hundred of their art works and have earned sixty awards in competitions. They have exhibited at the Los Angeles County Fair, the Music Center,

The unbelievable dresser has everything—sweat bands, headband and "40-love" underwear.

The equipment freak loses the match, runs down to the sporting goods store and buys another racket.

The trophy seeker's needs are so great that he'll lie to get into an event, claiming he's a C player when he's really a B.

The sensual kind of player has developed unbelievable extra movements in his serve.

The male chauvinist in mixed doubles delights in playing against women—and often is working out a lot of subconscious hostilities.

and the Pasadena Museum of Art. They have appeared on KNX-TV, "Steps to Learning," and have performed demonstration with Young Audiences of America, National Education Association Conferences, Youth Expression '73, and the Los Angeles Dance Theatre.

On one of their field trips, the youngsters went to a tennis court in Griffith Park in Los Angeles and were instructed to sketch what they saw. Upon returning to class, the children painted from their sketches. The results were amazing. The paintings captured the spontaneity and spirit of a tennis match. These paintings, done by children who knew little or nothing about tennis before being taken to a court, inspired these youngsters and could inspire others

to take a more active interest in the game. (A full account
of this project appears in "Through the Eyes of an Artist"
by Don Burgess, *Tennis West/East,* November 1973, pp.
24-27.)

THE IMPORTANCE OF PSYCHOLOGY

Volumes have been written about the art and technique of all kinds of sports—how to hold a club or racket,
how to strike a ball, timing, strokes—all the things that
might be called the anatomy of a particular sport. Relatively little, however, has been written about the psychology of sports. Psychology is particularly important in a
game like tennis, which pits one person against another, or
two against two. Many great talents in tennis have been
able to master all the fine techniques of the sport but have
never become great champions—because of foibles in their
own personality, their inability to recognize weaknesses in
their opponents, or their inability to size up psychological
situations during their matches.

This book will be devoted to the intangible, but to us
the most important aspect of tennis. We will not attempt
to present the technical aspects of personality theory, nor,
for that matter, complex techniques of therapy, psychoanalysis, behavior modification, ego psychology, or behavior conditioning. But what we will do is apply simple psychological principles to the game so that people who play
and watch tennis can understand and hopefully use them.

Probably the first and most important element in the
psychology of tennis is understanding yourself. This does
not mean undergoing psychoanalysis or psychotherapy, but
making an honest assessment of yourself *off* the tennis
court. Do you get flustered under stress? What kinds of
things upset you? Do you give vent to your emotions, or do
you repress them? If you repress them, does this interfere

with clear thinking? If you give vent to them, do they show in your facial expression or by your actions? Are you able to mask your feelings?

These and other aspects of your own personality dynamics underlie the whole psychology of tennis. Billie Jean King, the great tennis professional, feels that she became a complete tennis player when she gained a total awareness of herself and her game. "You have to understand yourself and know how to let off steam on the court and when to keep quiet."

The second element is your psychological assessment of your opponent. You should ask the same searching questions about your opponent as you ask of yourself. Billie Jean King is a master at analyzing her opponent. When she walks onto the court, she owns it, and she emits vibrations of self-possession. She has something analogous to what is known in the theater as stage presence. When a leading actor or actress walks onto the stage, he or she somehow demands attention, and the audience is immediately drawn. To Billie Jean King, the tennis court is like a stage, and often she exhibits what the audience may consider theatrics, but what are really both conscious and unconscious efforts at intimidating or upsetting her opponent. Immediately, as part of her act, she analyzes her opponent —particularly his or her weaknesses—and the match then becomes a physical and psychological event, as it does for all good players. In a match, the player who is tougher psychologically will not allow himself to become intimidated by anything.

Initially, it may seem that it would be much easier to size up yourself than your opponent, since obviously you have known yourself for much longer. This is not always so, however. It is not at all easy to look at yourself objectively, especially when it comes to personality dynamics. No one wants to see what are commonly known as his personality faults, but if you are to overcome these hindrances in order to achieve a successful game, you must face them squarely, analyze them, and see what can be done to overcome them.

You can get an idea of how a person plays tennis by observing how he drives a car. Like driving a car, playing tennis is a kind of projection that tells something about the way a person functions psychologically, especially in crucial situations. If you do not have advance information about the personality or behavior of your opponent, you may be able to size him up either in a warm-up or during the first few games. If he swears or throws his racket around, if he is disturbed by minor sights or sounds, if he gets fidgety or aggressive, these are signals or cues to you.

One of the important aspects of successful tennis play is concentration—the ability to blot out everything from your mind except what is going on in the confines of the court on which you are playing (photo 1). It is difficult in tennis, because there is always a tendency, even in great players, to think about such extraneous things as the sun, the wind, the audience, and other distractions that can interfere with effective playing. Players who lose their concentration very often resort to fantasies or daydreams about what happened the night before, various problems that are bothering them, or even their whole life situation. Nothing can be more detrimental to effective tennis than these kinds of fantasies. Only people who have effective defenses can overcome these temptations. Two seasoned tennis veterans who display the greatest concentration imaginable are Pancho Gonzales and Ken Rosewall. Although Gonzales has temperamental outbursts at times (partly due to a flair for showmanship that pleases the crowd), his concentration while playing is total. Practically nothing can distract Rosewall while he plays, perhaps a compensation for his relatively small stature.

PHOTO *1. Concentration is vital to good tennis play. You must be able to forget everything except the game.*

Egotism also may cause you to lose your concentration. Instead of thinking about what you are doing or what you are going to do, you think about what you look like or what the spectators are saying about you. Overconfidence, too, causes tennis players to lose their concentration, either when they play an opponent they think is greatly inferior or when they are so far ahead in a match they think it's in the bag. Remember that the underdog is always looking for a weakness in his opponent's armor. If you are overconfident and losing your ability to concentrate, and if your opponent notices, he will immediately take advantage. Remember that the match is never over until the last point is finished. When you are ahead, you should press even harder to win and finish than when you are behind. Very often when players build up a 5-0 lead in a set, they think it's impossible to lose; then they do just that—lose. Whenever you feel that you are losing your concentration, stop for a few seconds, look at your opponent, and think about the things you can do to beat him. Think of his weaknesses—if not his stroke weaknesses, then his psychological weaknesses.

When you play a tournament or match, it is always a good idea to "scout" your potential opponent or opponents. Observe the other players as they practice and play their matches. You should notice whether your potential opponent is aggressive and plays a "big game" or is a retriever like Bobby Riggs. Does he have a good overhand, lob, or drop shot? Is there a weakness in any of his strokes? What is his physical condition? Does he easily get upset on the court? If you don't have a chance to observe your opponent, you can get some inkling of his characteristics in the warm-up. There, of course, you must think fast.

If you're the kind of person who gets upset when you miss an easy shot, forget it; nothing will bring it back. Take a deep breath and think about the next point. Dwelling on a past mistake can cause your concentration to waver and usually results in a string of successive errors. The best thing to do is not to think about the point that has passed or the points in the future but the point that is being played *now*. A good way to help maintain concentration is to keep your eyes on what is going on within the tennis court and avoid looking at the surrounding scene. Another is to avoid thinking of the final outcome of your match, whether you are winning or losing.

About ten years ago, the British Tennis Association surveyed a random sample of the best tennis players of Great Britain, and 90 percent of those interviewed said that concentration was one of the most important attributes in tennis. Margaret Court, undoubtedly one of the greatest women tennis players who have ever lived, is prone at times to get nervous under pressure and to tend to lose her concentration. She has said that whenever she noticed her concentration was wandering, she would tell herself that since she could only think of one thing at a time, she would concentrate on *the ball*. That helped her overcome her nervousness.

Ms. Court suggests that a player, especially a tournament player who plays in front of crowds, should concentrate on watching the ball—not the opponent, the court, the crowd, or the relatives—and everything except the ball will disappear. If you do this, you will automatically prepare earlier and follow through on your strokes. In this way you will play the game point by point, and sometimes even forget the game or set score. By playing each point individually, it becomes easier psychologically to catch up when you are far behind.

Players find that when they "choke," it is very often because they are thinking ahead—fearing missing a shot or losing. In sports vernacular, choking is playing "super carefully." What happens is that you suddenly lose your confidence and dwell on the consequences of the match instead of concentrating on just watching and hitting the ball. Choking can also result in missing an easy shot or hitting the ball far out of the court from either overenthusiasm or loss of control of your nervous energy.

chapter two

"Gamesmanship"

Distractions are of two kinds—those on the court and those off the court.

ON-COURT DISTRACTIONS

On-court distractions come primarily from your opponent. Some opponents will go to great lengths and use all kinds of distractions to win. This is loosely known as "Gamesmanship," a term coined by Stephen Potter in his book *The Theory and Practice of Gamesmanship or The Art of Winning Games Without Actually Cheating*. Gamesmanship appears in many forms, but it is usually subtle. By definition, the gamesman deliberately sets out to put you off your game because he realizes that he is not good enough to win in any other way. One especially effective gambit of the gamesman is to hint that your etiquette or sportsmanship is in question. Or he may clown about or talk to you in the middle of the match or make some subtly derogatory remark when changing courts. The gamesman will talk to you about the quality of your game with such comments as "You're really not yourself today; you were much better the last time we played" or even "My, you're playing unusually well today."

The male author once played a match against a person who insisted on measuring the net height after each few points. If the net was a fraction of an inch high or low, he would insist on cranking it up or down. Although there is no rule against this, it is a distraction that interrupts the whole rhythm of the game. In another match, an opponent took between five and ten minutes to towel off in the interval between changing courts. Although there is a rule about this, it is rarely enforced, and this too interrupts the rhythm of the game. Another ploy is forgetting or changing the correct score. No matter what the distraction, if the gamesman's opponent becomes irritated, the gamesman takes great pains to apologize for being so negligent.

A distraction that bothers more people than one might think is the attire and appearance of the opponent. Odd pants or shorts, clashing colors and patterns, unmatching socks, weird hairdos, and so on all can upset a sensitive player. (The usual attire for tennis players, of course, is all white, and until recently white was prescribed at most tournaments. The loosening of color restrictions gives the gamesman a greater opportunity for distraction within the accepted range of tennis clothing.)

One player went to the extreme of drawing blood by hitting himself on the leg with his racket. (In addition to distracting the opponent, this ploy is meant to get the sympathy of the audience for the "injured" player.)

Other ploys designed to make you lose your concentration include the subtle one of choosing "side" instead of serving when the racket is spun to decide "side" or "serve." The winner may select "side," and the person who is to serve may wonder why he did this and whether his own serve is adequate. This may in turn affect the server's service game. Then there is the player who walks onto the court with eight rackets—a subtle method of intimidation—and the foreign player who says he is the champion of some country that no one has ever heard of.

The size of an opponent can also be a distraction. The sight of a huge person across the net can wear you down psychologically, and the sight of a very small one can give you a lift, since you may think he is an easy mark. Although size may be an advantage in tennis, particularly in doubles, it is not always so by any means. Some of the greatest players in the history of the game have been average or below average in size. Witness Bitsy Grant, a great player in the 1930s and 1940s; Chuck McKinley, a Davis Cup player in the 1950s and 1960s; Rosemary Casals, currently ranked among the top ten women players; and Ken Rosewall, one of Australia's great players.

Another distraction may be your opponent's style of play, especially if he uses one or more unorthodox shots. Many of the players on the all-woman Virginia Slims circuit have difficulty with Francoise Durr, the great French player, because of her unconventional game (photo 2). Ms. Durr has a peculiar habit of looking one way and hitting the ball the other, so her opponent is likely to miss a shot if he or she is watching Ms. Durr instead of watching the ball. She also has an unconventional way of hitting the ball on all her shots.

One time when everyone's concentration wavers is on an "off day." Even the great players have days when nothing seems to work and everything goes wrong (photo 3). Your timing is off when you volley; your backhand is atrocious; and your first serve simply will not go in. Naturally, your opponent is having one of his good days. You know you can beat him under ordinary circumstances, but today is

PHOTO 2. *Many players on the Virginia Slims circuit have diffi-culty playing Francoise Durr because of her unorthodox game.*

PHOTO 3. *Once in a while everyone has an "off day" when nothing works and everything goes wrong.*

different. You get angrier and angrier. Every bone in your body aches with the knowledge that you are taking a beating from someone you know you can beat ninety-nine times out of a hundred. You're furious; you look it; and you begin to act it, too. You start hitting the ball all over the place—mostly into the net, at the sidelines, and over the fence.

The first thing to do under those circumstances is to stop letting your annoyance show. Every time you tear your hair, it only encourages your opponent. He will probably play better than usual simply because he knows you are frustrated and angry. As you lose confidence, he gains it. So try to calm yourself. Try to analyze what you are doing wrong, and at the same time slow down the tempo of the game a little. Slowing down when you're being beaten is analogous to what a fighter does in a clinch, what a lawyer does when he asks for an adjournment, what a basketball team does when it asks for a time out. When things get hectic, try a pause. You can't legitimately or ethically ask for a time out during a tennis match, but you *can* legitimately and ethically walk a little more slowly to pick up a ball, or take a little more time before serving in order to gather your wits. Sometimes slowing down and *acting* calm will become infectious, and you will settle down and *become* calm.

Taking a reasonable time between points should not be confused with stalling. Every player has his own rhythm and timing between points. Some players like to play very fast without much time between points, almost as if they want to get the match over with as soon as possible. Some players simply like to take their time, and this preference has nothing to do with stalling. Sometimes it is good, legitimate, and effective strategy to speed up or slow down the game deliberately. Hopefully, a change of pace—not just taking time between points but also hitting soft, deep shots during the game—will throw your opponent off. Likewise, if you find that you're tired, take your time between points or slow the game down by hitting a few deep lobs until you can catch your breath.

Another distracting habit of some players is bouncing the ball sharply eight or ten times before serving. The talented Jimmy Connors has a habit of doing this. Undoubtedly the bouncing is unintentional, but it is distracting to his opponents. Other habits that are bothersome include tying shoelaces or straightening the racket strings after each point or looking intently at the strings after missing a shot. Blaming the racket for missing a point is technically known as *projection* (photo 4). While projection can be a healthy defense mechanism that often prevents depression, a tennis player will rarely find anything wrong

PHOTO 4. *Blaming your racket for missing a point is technically known as projection.*

with the racket. This blaming of an inanimate object can tend to become a habit and interfere with improvement of your game, because it prevents you from recognizing the real problem. Tom Okker, the great Dutch player, has an involuntary habit of straightening his strings after a point. Glaring at the umpire or linesman to intimidate him is another distraction, and Ion Tiriac, the Rumanian player, has a penchant for doing this.

The method of serving is another of the countless tactics in gamesmanship. In tennis, there are no pre-scribed rules for serving, except where the server must stand. Many players, in order to upset their opponents, will underslice or undercut the serve instead of serving the usual overhead way. They will serve underhand and slice the ball so that when it lands on the other side of the net, it will bounce sideways or backward. Experienced players who have reasonably quick reflexes can see such a serve coming and can either return it normally or put it away. Some players give such a server a dose of his own medicine and slice it back to the original server—much to his sur-prise. The last thing to do is appear upset at an undercut or slice serve, since this is undoubtedly the precise effect that the culprit wants. If this does upset you, do a little slow-ing down and walk around with the ball in your hand to calm yourself. If you are upset, you should try not to show it, since your opponent will continue his tactics as long as he knows they will throw you off. Julie Heldman, a leading tennis professional, has become a master of the underhand serve. She uses it to slow down and change the pace of a match and also to catch her opponent off guard.

Another ploy that may catch some people off guard is not to give your opponent much time to prepare for the service return. Some servers do this deliberately to speed up the game or when they feel their opponents are taking too long. If the receiver attempts to return the serve even though he was not ready, he will have to convince the umpire of that. If a player is returning a serve and is not fully ready for the serve, he should not attempt to hit it back. He should merely raise his arm and not move at all; he is then legitimately telling his opponent not to serve so fast. This can become a form of psychological warfare over which player is in control of the pace of the match and which one must withstand pressure from his opponent.

A word should be said here about umpires and linesmen. Umpires, linesmen, referees, and tournament officials are chosen because of their supposed knowledge of the game and their acute eyesight. Umpires and linesmen are human, however, and do make errors. In general (although there has been a great deal of dispute about this), they serve without compensation and are subject to vociferous abuse from both players and audience. Sometimes whatever they do seems to be wrong, and occasionally some gamesmen will glare, swear, or even refuse to play when they think a bad call has been made against them. Of course, umpires and linesmen are not used except in tournaments, and even in many sanctioned tournaments—those approved by the United States (Lawn) Tennis Association—there are no linesmen. Some top-flight tournament players seem to harass linesmen perennially—for example, Rumania's Ion Tiriac and Australia's Bob Hewitt (now living in South Africa). They do this either because of their excitable nature or to gain an advantage at the moment in a disputed call by bullying the linesmen so that future balls will be called their way. Such bullying is of course disconcerting to the opponent. Linesmen not only judge whether balls are in or out, but also judge foot faults—whether the server steps over the base line when serving. This can also get to be a psychological game. In a professional women's

match once, Wendy Overton was playing Valerie Ziegen-
fuss. The foot-fault judge repeatedly called Ms. Overton for
foot-faulting, whereupon she finally disputed the judgment,
asking exactly how far she had stepped over the base line,
the positions of her feet, and so on. Obviously she thought
the linesman was wrong. Then the linesman, probably intimidated, stopped his calls, and the center linesman, sens-
ing what was going on, started to call foot faults. Ms. Overton promptly stopped foot-faulting.

These psychological games go on all the time between players and linesmen, and the disputes arise more
often from personality clashes between players and linesmen than from actual fault calls. Most linesmen do a con-
scientious job, but occasionally a linesman may have an
unconscious bias toward one or more of the players, in
which case his perception may be distorted. If you are
playing in a match and you feel a particular linesman is
making bad calls against you, you should appeal to the
umpire for decisions. If you are playing in a tournament
and you feel that your opponent is making unfair calls
and there is no linesman present, you should ask the tournament director to find a linesman. Nothing is more disconcerting than having either a linesman or an opponent
consistently make decisions that you consider wrong. Some
players develop a kind of paranoia at close line decisions.
Some feel they "never get a break," so they in turn seldom
give their opponents any breaks either.

Junior players (age eighteen and under) have sometimes been known to cheat in tournaments because of parental pressure. So much pressure may be put on a youngster to win that unfair play seems the only resort. This
should warn parents whose youngsters play in tournaments
—let them do the best they can without facing guilt feelings
if they lose.

The Southern California Tennis Association adopted an Honor Code of Ethics that is sent to each member and posted at every sanctioned tournament. The introduction reads: "The Southern California Tennis Association adopted this Honor Code of Ethics in order that all followers of tennis will know what is expected of them as players and as spectators and thereby enhance the enjoyment of this wonderful game by everyone." Part of the code deals specifically with line calling. If an opponent is causing trouble, the proper thing to do is to ask for a linesman; if a linesman is causing trouble, ask the umpire for a decision. Only on very rare occasions should linesmen be replaced, and you should not directly ask the linesmen to leave. You should remember that in the heat of battle, perceptions tend to become distorted, especially to someone who is in constant motion. You are bound to see shots the way you want to see them rather than as they are, and the chances are that an unbiased linesman can see shots better than you.

If you are playing before an audience, you should remember that on a neutral court the audience usually favors the underdog. On a questionable line call in favor of the favorite, the audience will jeer; but on one in favor of the underdog, they will cheer. There is also a tendency, although not universal, for some linesmen to take the word of the better player on a questionable call. In many instances linesmen and umpires probably think that the better player could have made the shot and that the lesser player probably would have missed it. It is logical to believe that the better player makes fewer mistakes than the lesser one, and this attitude may carry over in calling some matches and interfere with a linesman's perception on close calls.

In match play, knowing that you have a good linesman and a good umpire gives you a feeling of confidence.

The tournament player knows that when he has a good linesman and a good umpire, he will be more likely to take chances and try hitting closer to the line. When a tournament player has incompetent linesmen and umpires, he is reluctant to take chances by trying to hit very close to the line for fear of an unfavorable call. In some rare instances, players try to get people with whom they are friendly to be a linesman or an umpire. While the umpire or linesman will try to be fair, the players know that the official may unconsciously favor his friend because he wants him to win. Thus, it is obviously a poor idea for friends to call matches. Ball boys and ball girls also have their favorites, and their reactions to the players may affect the match.

Most tennis today is played at clubs or in public parks. These social matches—whether played for pride or for a next higher position on the ladder—usually are not officiated. Both players keep score and call their own lines. At times, delicate situations arise and may upset one or both of the players. For example, one of the rules in tennis is to let the ball bounce before calling it "out." In social tennis, however, it is acceptable to catch the ball before it bounces if it is obviously going well out of bounds. Some people catch the ball even when it is very doubtful whether or not it would have been out. This tactic is distracting and unnerving to say the least. If someone tries it on you, simply ask to replay the point. Many people are reluctant to ask for a replay because it implies that they doubt the judgment of their opponent. If you feel strongly that your opponent is catching good balls, however, you have a right to replay the point.

Another irritating kind of opponent is the perennial pusher or lobber. This person will continually simply cream puff, hit the ball softly, or continually lob it no matter what you do. Technically, you should come up to the net and try to pulverize the lob so that your opponent will not be able to return the shot. In situations of this kind, however, you will probably have a tendency to be overanxious and over-hit the ball or to come to the net too soon. Such tactics by opponents are extremely annoying and distracting (which is exactly the effect your opponent wants), and they result in the loss of your concentration.

Instead of slowing up the game by lobbing, you or your opponent can speed up the game. Speeding up the game, however, is not so much a part of gamesmanship as is continually lobbing or stalling on the court. It is part of legitimate tactics, although quick-serving is not. Just how much time should take place between the end of a point and the beginning of the next point is a moot question. It is common courtesy to wait until your opponent is ready before serving, but some players will take advantage when their opponent is slow to get in position or has been maneuvered out of the court and cannot get back into position to receive the serve immediately. Thus, the serve will whiz right past him if served before he is ready. Such maneuvers are upsetting, and if you are playing in a match, you should complain to the umpire; if you are not in a match, you should tell your opponent not to serve until you are ready, and that you will tell him when you are ready.

Certain strategies can be used when returning a serve. If your opponent has a hard serve, it may be a good idea to take a few steps back while keeping alert for any change of pace in the serve. If your opponent has a poor first serve and an even poorer second serve, it is wise to take a few steps forward and attack on the return. Standing close to the service line may make your opponent nervous. He may be afraid he will double-fault, or he might be afraid of hitting the ball too softly because he thinks you will slam it back. Or he may feel the pressure to hit his second serve harder than normal so he may miss and double-fault instead, simply because you added pressure by taking a few steps forward. A receiver also can try to fake out the server by waiting to one side of the service square favoring either the forehand or the backhand return. By standing toward one side, the receiver tempts the server to hit to the opposite side, to which the receiver will automatically go. A receiver also may start moving and jump around while the server starts his serving motion. Another strategy that may disconcert your opponent is to drop-shot your opponent's serve when he stands well in back of the base line. This usually will be done on the second serve, and the drop shot must be unexpected and disguised. Bobby Riggs did this well in his celebrated defeat of Margaret Court in 1973. Rosemary Casals also is adept at this.

In tournament play, it is a good idea to arrive a few days early if you will be playing in a different climate, time zone, or altitude or on a surface to which you are not accustomed. You should also inquire about the type of ball to be used, since not all balls play the same or last the same length of time. In any case, you should remember that your opponent is playing under the same natural conditions as you are. Quite often it is *not* the most skillful player who ends up winning a match but the one who adjusts better to difficult and different conditions.

The distractions and examples of gamesmanship just discussed are not quite the same as the legitimate tactics of maneuvering your opponent in and out of position. Tennis tactics are very much like those of chess and many are psychological in nature. Let us take several concrete examples in tennis. If you want to tire your opponent, you should remember that it is easier to tire one who is running

up and down the court than one who is running from side
to side. In addition, most players are weaker hitters after
turning than they are remaining straight.

A universal axiom in tennis is to maintain as much
pressure on your opponent as possible during every part of
the match. The trick in this psychological maneuvering is
to get on top and stay on top, consistent with your physical conditioning. One of the ways of maintaining pressure
is to rush the net as much as possible. However, this is
physically tiring, so that in a long match (best of five sets),
it is probably best to come to the net *primarily* on your
serve. While maintaining this pressure, you should try to
pace yourself as much as possible. Some players adopt the
psychological strategy in a five-set match of attacking
fiercely at the net during the first two sets. Then, if they win
these and feel they are tiring in the second set, they recharge
their batteries in the next two sets and concentrate on the
fifth one. The danger, of course, is that if you are not
able to recover, you will not have strength for the crucial fifth set. However, many top players employ this kind
of psychological strategy. When you feel yourself getting
tired, it is not advisable to run for impossible shots. You
may save that point, but the effort may cost you the next
two games. Thus, conserving your energy and knowing your
energy reserves and capabilities are extremely important.
Stamina is vital in tennis.

Another element of overall psychological maneuvering
is deception. Deception is simply giving the wrong cues to
your opponent or sending messages that will throw him off
balance. For example, an alert player will notice where his
opponent stands to serve. Often when serving, a player will
stand in one spot on the base line if he intends the ball to go
to his opponent's forehand, and in another if he intends it to
go to his backhand. As server, if you see your opponent

shift position according to where you stand when you serve, you should mix up your positions—that is, serve to different places from different positions. One of the great masters of deception in serving is Arthur Ashe, who gives no clues as to where he will hit the ball and changes his serve depending on where his opponent stands to receive it. This tactic, combined with his amazingly hard serve, makes his serve at times unbeatable. Another method of deception, mentioned earlier, is looking one place and hitting to another. Of course, this takes a great amount of control, since players do not always look in the same direction in which they hit the ball. Looking in another direction from where the ball will go is probably more effective during the course of playing a point than it is while serving. To a lesser extent, you can deceive your opponent by the height and position to which you toss the ball when serving, since many players watch the toss of the ball to try to determine where the server will hit it.

Allied to gamesmanship are the excuses made by the loser of a match. Such excuses include the following:

1. "It was too windy."
2. "The sun was directly overhead."
3. "I wear glasses and can't see because of glare and fogging up."
4. "My good racket is being repaired."
5. "My new shoes hurt my feet. I needed new shoes because it was slippery and I didn't want to risk injury." Or "I didn't have time to buy a new pair of shoes, so I couldn't run well because the soles are too smooth."
6. "I had a tennis elbow [or bad knees, blisters, a sore shoulder, or pulled stomach muscles]."
7. "I stayed out till 5 A.M. What can you expect with a hangover and no sleep?"

8. "I haven't practiced since last time we played, which was at least six months ago."
9. "I just recovered from flu [or pneumonia, or another serious ailment]."
10. "I just ate and had a stomach ache."
11. "I don't like heavy-duty balls [or can't see white balls]."
12. "You played unusually well; I can beat you nineteen times out of twenty."
13. "You're so lucky with your mis-hit and let shots."
14. "There were too many bad bounces."
15. "The courts were too fast [or too slow]. I'm used to other courts."
16. "You've been playing for a much longer time than I have."
17. "You've been taking lessons for years and I'm self-taught."
18. "You're ten years younger. Wait till you reach my age."
19. "You gave me too many bad calls."

OFF-COURT DISTRACTIONS

Now let's take a look at distractions that originate off the court. These are primarily of two types: environmental and human. Environmental conditions include such things as the altitude, climate, and weather, including the sun, lighting, wind, rain, rustling of leaves, and noises from airplanes or automobiles. Human factors include the audience and other people who may be watching the match, excluding those directly involved—linesmen, ball boys, umpires, referees, and so on. Seasoned players learn to play in all kinds of conditions since they are forced to adapt quite readily not only to different surfaces but also to different levels of temperature, altitude, wind, sun, and so forth.

Heat and humidity can be a serious problem for tennis players in some countries and during certain seasons. In the United States, for example, during the summer tennis season, valleys and inland regions are much warmer and wetter than coastal areas, and good players can be overcome by heat and humidity. The female author learned to play tennis in San Francisco and had severe difficulty adjusting to the seasons when she first went on tour. Altitude, too, can affect play. When players from the United States compete in Mexico City, for example, they have difficulty catching their breath. In addition, balls have a tendency to "float" in higher altitudes. Players who compete internationally must contend with the fact that the seasons are reversed in the Southern Hemisphere. When it is winter in North America and Europe, it is summer in Australia, where tennis is also very popular.

Those who are used to playing in a variety of conditions, particularly heat and humidity, have a distinct psychological advantage over those who are not. The seasoned player will quickly see that his opponent is wilting because of the weather and will run him all the harder. Some players question the ethics involved, but it is perfectly legitimate to take advantage of the weather.

You can help overcome the disadvantage of hot, humid weather in several ways. One is to wear a sponge sweatband on your forehead to prevent perspiration from running into your eyes or onto your glasses. A wide-brimmed hat will protect you against the sun, help absorb perspiration, and hold the sweatband in place. Perspiration can be prevented from dropping onto the hand holding the racket by an absorbent wristband, or it can be wiped off with a towel. Powdered resin can be rubbed on the handle of the racket to help keep it from slipping. On hot, humid days, make your opponent move more than you do, hitting short lobs and shots from side to side.

In addition to creating heat and humidity, the sun has a psychological effect. Glaring sunlight can affect three specific shots—a serve, an overhead, and a lob—and indirectly affect a person's whole game. If you see that your opponent is bothered by the sun and that it is in his eyes, you might try lobbing consistently and see what happens. If this is done to you, it is best to abandon the lob and let the ball bounce first and then hit it.

The opposite of glaring sun is too little light—a problem that can occur if a match is extended into the evening or if a sudden storm comes up and darkens the sky. Inability to see the ball can be a distinct physical and psychological hazard, and it is perfectly legitimate to ask for postponement of a match due to poor lighting or darkness. (This is less a problem than it used to be, because many colored balls, particularly yellow ones, are in use and are easy to see.) Lighting also can be a problem on an indoor court. Artificial lighting may be uneven, or one light might shine directly in your face when you are on one side of the court. The best type of lighting for tennis is indirect—the lights are reflected against the ceiling, so light is more evenly distributed in the court area. With indirect lighting, it is impossible to "lose" the ball against a bright bulb.

Tangential to lighting are shadows that cross the court as the sun changes position during the day. It is particularly disconcerting for a player continually to come out of a shadow into the sun or light and then go back into the shadow again.

Another element that can influence a person's game is a strong wind. Wind can blow in three directions—with you, against you, or across the court. Sometimes the wind will seem to blow in three directions at once! When playing in the wind, it is best to maintain a good attitude and realize that your opponent is playing under the same conditions. Usually playing in the wind gives an advantage to the underdog or lesser player because it serves as an equalizer. The better player will not usually play as well in the wind since he must "ungroove," or change the rhythm and timing of his strokes. Sometimes playing with a lighter racket will help because it can be difficult to stroke the ball in the wind. Try to ascertain whether the wind is blowing steadily in one direction or whether it is unpredictable and gusty. When the wind is blowing in one direction you can compensate for it and change your stroke according to the direction of the wind.

When wind does come up, don't fight it, but make it work to your advantage. Hit the ball with less force than usual when the wind is with you and with more than usual when the wind is against you. When the wind is against you, exploit the lob, since the wind will do all sorts of tricks with the ball and upset your opponent's equilibrium. Furthermore, no matter how hard you hit it, the ball will seem to stay in the court. On the other hand, lobbing *with* the wind can be dangerous, since it seems that no matter how softly you hit it, there is a tendency for the ball to go out of bounds. When playing with the wind, it may be advantageous to come to the net often, since your opponent's shots may not have the speed they would have if he were not playing against the wind. On service, try to keep the ball toss low; otherwise it can get carried away. The higher the ball goes, the more the wind will blow it. This is especially so with very high lobs.

Another group of distractions, already mentioned, is noises, both on the court and off the court—airplanes, trains, autos, rustling trees, barking dogs, meowing cats,

chirping birds, and so on. Sometimes even the smell of pol-
luted air coming from a nearby factory can be distracting.
If you are concentrating on your game, however, you will
be less aware of these things around you. The trick, when
you hear, smell, or otherwise sense these distractions, is to
think of your tennis technique—how you are controlling
your shots, what the other person is doing wrong—and blot
out from your mind the extraneous stimuli.

In regard to human noises, such as from the audience,
Billie Jean King says, "I'm definitely in the minority with
my fellow players on the subject of yelling at tennis matches.
I say let the crowd roar if a good shot turns them on. After
all, without paying customers, you have no pro sports. Yelling wouldn't bother my concentration, but some of the
others think it would bother theirs. But as I told them, they'd
adjust to it."

Some players do not adjust to it, however. Tennis
audiences are no different from other sports audiences, and
all kinds of people make a crowd. There are hecklers who
seem to enjoy making all kinds of noise. There are advis-
ers who know everything about the game and keep advising
one or another player what to do (from the side lines).
There are the perennial home-town rooters who will cheer
when the local player makes a good shot and when his opponent makes a poor one. Vociferous applauders clap,
whistle, stomp their feet, and yell.

It is not easy to ignore some of these. Arthur Larsen,
a top player some years ago, actually went into the audience
during a match in Australia and threatened to punch a fan
in the nose because of his heckling. At a tennis match in
Sacramento, California, where Eric Van Dillen played
Clark Graebner, the audience was strongly partisan in Van
Dillen's favor because he was a Californian. Every time
Graebner made a poor shot, the audience laughed. Graeb-

ner, not noted for his equanimity, finally let his temper get out of control and screamed, "What is so funny? That is not funny at all." The crowd stopped laughing.

Of course, the average player does not have to contend with a paying audience, but those who play in sanctioned tournaments very often do. The more one gets used to playing before an audience, the more one adjusts to all kinds of spectators. It is quite difficult not to become disheartened during a match when the audience is not on your side. The audience can provide a great deal of moral support and encouragement. When playing before an audience, you must try to be deaf to unfavorable comments. You should learn not to become self-conscious when people are watching. It is fear of failure that causes players to behave self-consciously in front of an audience. Although Margaret Court has played all over the world, in front of all kinds of people, whenever she gets behind in a match in front of a crowd, her fear of failure causes her to become self-conscious and get the jitters. On the other hand, "attention lovers" seem to play better when more people are watching. For example, Chris Evert played extraordinarily well in her Forest Hills, New York, debut at the age of sixteen because the crowd was pulling for her. American players have repeatedly complained about unruly and biased spectators and officials in Italy, France, and Rumania.

More and more youngsters are playing tennis in the junior ranks (photo 5). Tournaments abound throughout the country and the world for juniors. Very often parents go along with the youngsters, and parents can scarcely be called a nonpartisan and disinterested group. Exhortations, advice, and coaching from the side lines are an annoying but not uncommon practice among parents whose youngsters are playing in a tournament. Many "tennis parents" may pick their children up every day at school to take them to practice, drive to far away tournaments on weekends, and so so. Very often, parents of "seeded" players in a tournament make unusual demands of tournament officials such as asking that their youngster be given a court to practice on any time the youngster desires. (For details of seeding see Appendix A, "Rules for Seeding the Draw.") Many children may want their parents to order their lives, but often a child star is pushed hard by overambitious parents who try to live through their children. Sometimes a youngster does not have the ability to be the champion the parents expect, and he or she simply loses interest. Parents should be on guard against this sometimes unconscious but human parental foible.

Even parents of older players follow them in tournaments. Sometimes a parent may actually go right onto the court to give advice to a budding champion. The Southern

PHOTO 5. *Increasing numbers of youngsters are playing tennis in the junior ranks. Note that these courts are reserved for students.*

California Tennis Association Honor Code says, "It is discourteous and distracting for parents, friends or coaches to volunteer advice on line calls, scoring, or the conduct of the match except during the official rest period that is allowed between second and third sets. Gross unfairness should be reported to the tournament director."

Just what to do about overexuberant parents is a difficult question. Maternal and paternal instincts are quite strong, and if prohibitions are placed on parental exhortations, they must be done with tact and diplomacy. One rule is cardinal in tournaments. No parents are allowed to sit next to each other when their offspring are playing against each other.

When tennis is the youngster's primary outlet and activity, his attempts to achieve good results in tournaments are his way of gaining approval from his parents. On the other hand, some parents act as managers who have outlived their roles. These men and women are sadly unaware they no longer are needed as protectors and organizers for their children.

chapter three

Court Strategy

We will now discuss in depth the whole psychology of court strategy, although some of the tactics have already been alluded to in the previous chapters. (For a diagram and dimensions of the tennis court, see Appendix B.)

Again, it is not the purpose or intent of this book to discuss the technique of various strokes, but to offer suggestions about how and when to make certain strokes more effective. The first and most important element of court strategy is to be aggressive and bold and play to win. Hit the ball with confidence and take charge of the game as soon as possible. The key to winning tennis is the ability to control the match, and controlling the match depends not only on effective strokes but also on your state of mind. If you feel that you are going to win and your actions show it, your attitude doubtless will have an effect on your opponent.

SERVE

On fast courts today, the service is almost always followed to the net by the server. The service is the only stroke with which the receiver initially has nothing to do (photo 6). As server, you simply stand with the ball in one hand, the racket in the other. You need not hurry, and you can survey the situation on the court at your leisure. This is the time to concentrate on putting in a strong, deep serve and running up to the net behind it. In closing right in, you build up your own feelings of aggression and confidence while having the reverse effect on the receiver. While you should not try this deliberately, thundering hooves running behind the serve can have a demoralizing effect on your opponent.

Deciding where you want to place the serve also is an important psychological and technical weapon. Try not to give away your intentions by standing in a certain spot or by looking at the spot where you intend to serve. Exactly where you will serve will depend on a number of factors, primarily the weakness or strength of your opponent. If he or she has an overpowering forehand, do not send your serve to the forehand. Any one kind of serve, if used repeatedly, can lose its effectiveness. Variety keeps the receiver guessing and off balance, but avoid letting your serves, however varied, fall into a pattern. If you get into the habit of hard slice kick serves, your opponent will soon catch on. "Overpressing," or hitting forcefully, deep, and hard, is a common cause of faulting. The way to avoid it is to take your time in serving, because the service is the only time you have to settle into a position, survey the court completely, and think about what you are going to do.

The second serve also can be a powerful psychological weapon. The objective of the second serve, which is usually hit with a slice and spin, is to get the ball in play. It's a good idea to hit the second serve squarely in front of your opponent, because this placement in a sense immobilizes him. The slice is a good weapon as a change of pace and will often surprise your opponent. Many people try to overhit their second serve because they are afraid of a very strong return. Consequently these people have a tendency to double-fault. Double-faulting obviously gives an edge to your opponent, for if you fail to hit a wide area from a stationary position the two times you serve, you are literally giving the point to your opponent without his having to work for it.

PHOTO 6. *The service is the only stroke with which the opponent has nothing to do initially.*

It is very important to get at least 60 percent of your first serves in the service box. Serving is very tiring, and thus if you keep missing your first serves, you must serve twice as many balls and work twice as hard.

Practicing a certain deception in the serve, as mentioned in the previous chapter, is probably as important as in any other stroke. Deception can be practiced in both the first and second serves. You can hit the ball into different corners at different speeds, using different types of serves, but sometimes with the same body stance. The receiver may anticipate several different moves, but he never knows which one is coming. Of course, this takes a great deal of control. Giving a false cue is another excellent method of deception. For example, while serving in the deuce court—the right-hand service court box where the deuce point is played—the server may nod his head slightly in the direction of the center line, and move his racket slightly forward in the direction of the center line, but actually hit the ball to the opposite side of the court.

The toss of the ball is very often a clue to the direction and type of service. Experienced receivers look to see how and where the server tosses the ball to anticipate the kind of serve to expect. For the slice serve, most people toss the ball slightly to the right of the head and the front of the body. For the flat serve, the ball is tossed over the head. For the American twist, the ball is tossed to the left of the head. Thus, if a player can make these serves with only a slight difference in the ball toss, his serve will probably deceive his opponent. The height to which you toss the ball in serving may be another factor. The longer the ball is in the air, the more clues the receiver is likely to get to the direction of the ball and the type of serve.

Many professional coaches believe that the best serve is to the opponent's backhand. Although this is not always true, it is a good general rule. If your opponent has a poor forehand, serve there—keeping in mind, of course, that you should mix up your serves so your opponent will not automatically expect a serve in the same spot each time. You should also vary the speed and spin of your serves. This prevents the receiver from getting too accustomed to a certain pace. Some players have an easier time with a hard, flat serve. In this case, slow your serve down to about three-quarters speed, which may be enough to throw your opponent off and force him to generate his own pace on the return.

RETURNING THE SERVE

There are certain strategies you can use while returning the serve. Generally, the service return is an improvised ground stroke. You usually don't have time to take a full swing—only time to block or jab at the ball. Thus, going for a winning point on a service return may look spectacular when it comes off, but is not a percentage shot. If your opponent has a very long, hard serve, it may be a good idea to take a few steps backward, but you should be alert for any serves that indicate a change of pace. If your opponent has a soft first serve, and an even softer second serve, then it is a good idea to take a few steps forward and attack on the return. Standing quite close to the service line, especially after your opponent misses his first serve, may make him nervous. He's afraid that he'll double-fault, or he's afraid that he'll hit the second serve too softly, or he may feel pressure to hit his second serve harder than normal because you added a little bit of pressure by taking a few steps forward.

A receiver can tell when a server is getting nervous. The clue will inevitably show in the toss of the ball. Some players toss the ball higher and higher the more important the serve, and others simply toss it more wildly. Some players rush their downward service swing as if to get the point completed as soon as possible. Another stratagem that was mentioned earlier is to drop-shot the second serve. It is almost never done on the first serve, only on the second. The drop shot is not effective, however, unless it is disguised and unexpected. Otherwise your opponent will be halfway up to the net before the ball has come off your racket. As a general rule, you should not drop-shot to someone who rushes the net after every serve.

The Volley

The volley is extremely important in tennis psychology because it is the medium of attack. The ball does not bounce during a volley, and the play is usually hard and fast. It used to be thought that volleying should be learned only after ground strokes were mastered. Now the teaching philosophy is to learn volleying at the same time as learning ground strokes. Thus, instead of staying back and hitting what used to be the better ground strokes, a player learns to become more mobile and can attempt both ground strokes and volleying at the same time.

A volley is basically a reflex shot that is anticipated. The trick in the volley is to watch the ball very closely and not be concerned about where your opponent is. You should watch your opponent only if you have plenty of time. Even if you see that your opponent is standing where you are planning to hit the ball, don't worry. Hit the ball there, but make certain you hit it well. Even though your opponent may guess where the ball is going, chances are that he will miss the return if you hit it deep and hard enough. Since you must react quickly, don't change your mind unless you have plenty of time. Many mistakes and points lost are caused by indecision as to where one should hit the ball.

Since the volley should be played from close to the net whenever possible, coming to and being at the net will most upset your opponent.

You will notice that top players invariably follow their serves to the net and, when possible, charge to the net at any other time they think it feasible. Remember that the first psychological axiom in tennis is to be aggressive and take charge of the match. This can best be done with an effective serve and volley. The closer to the net you come to make your shots, the better you are able to attack.

The volley may also be an effective weapon on courts that have an uneven surface, such as grass. Because the ball does not bounce in the volley, on surfaces where there is the possibility of a bad bounce, you have more confidence to volley. The effectiveness of the volley on grass or hard courts is shown by Billie Jean King's mastery over Chris Evert on grass, and Evert's mastery over King on clay, where the backcourt game is more effective.

In line with this psychological weapon of attack, always move forward after the first volley; do not stand still, and do not go backward. This is advisable from both psychological and technical viewpoints. Technically, by moving closer to the net, you increase the number of angles at which you can hit the ball; psychologically, this may upset your opponent.

It may be easier to volley on a windy day than to hit a ground stroke if you have a choice, because the volley cuts the ball off before it takes off in the wind current. However, you must watch the ball carefully and be able to adjust your strokes to take the wind into account and be prepared to make sudden changes when the wind shifts or blows very hard.

Don't try to kill the first volley unless you have an extremely easy ball to hit. It's best to maneuver your oppo-

nent and not try for the put-away shot—a clear winner
that the opponent is unable to return—until the second or
third volley. Of course, one of the really great psychological weapons is the stop volley. A large number of stop volleys, like effective drop shots, will simply demoralize an
opponent. Cecilia Martinez ended one of the great matches
of her career—her victory over Virginia Wade, the great
English player, to reach the quarter finals of the 1970
Wimbledon tournament—with a stop volley. (Stop volleys
can also be called advance finesse shots and should not be
attempted by beginners or unless you have a complete
mastery of the volley. They should not be used unless your
opponent is well behind the base line.)

The volley is extremely important in doubles, and a
competent volleyer is a great asset to a doubles team.
Doubles will be discussed in more detail later. A player
without a good volley is severely limited in his or her use
of court strategy. These short swings are more important
in tennis psychology than most people think. Another important psychological shot, which requires a great deal of
skill, is the lob volley—hitting a lob off a volley when both
you and your opponent are at the net. It is probably most
frequently used in doubles.

The Lob

The lob is one of the most underrated shots in tennis psychology. Offensively, one of its purposes is to break
the rhythm of your opponent's game. Its greatest effectiveness is in the beginning of a match, when your opponent
may not yet be warmed up and may not yet be comfortable hitting overheads. Furthermore, his or her timing
probably is not yet at its peak. At this stage, it is strategi-
cally important to intersperse lobs with ground strokes; when
your opponent is just getting the rhythm of hitting your

lobs and is interrupted with ground strokes, he will have to reestablish his entire rhythm.

Bill Russell, the great basketball player and coach, once said, "Basketball is a game of habit. If you make a player deviate from his habit by 'psyching' him, you've got him." This is even more true of tennis than of basketball, and the one stroke with which you can really upset your opponent's habits is the lob! The average player doesn't lob for a variety of reasons. First, many players who are beginning the game want to go all-out and try to overwhelm their opponent at once. They think they cannot do this with the lob. As a matter of fact, the average player thinks the lob is a "sissy" shot. You will seldom find a top-ranked player, however, who doesn't have a good lob. One woman professional on the Virginia Slims tour confided that although she knew she could win more points by continuous lobbing, she didn't always resort to it because it "looked bad." Even a good volleyer is likely to have an erratic overhead because it is seldom tested by returning lobs.

It's a good idea to test your opponent with a lob to see what he or she does; this will give you an idea of what to do next. You should observe whether your opponent smashes them deep or angles them softly at the side lines. If he smashes them, this is your cue to stay behind the base line so that you can retrieve the shot if it is good. If he tries to catch you with an angle shot, then stay in close to the net. In the warm-up, you should test your opponent's overhead to see if it is weak or strong, and if you detect a weak overhead, lob him or her consistently and persistently.

Lobs, like other shots, should be used in special and strategic situations, especially when you can surprise your opponent. For example, when the game score is your advantage, your opponent might think that you will not lob, so you might try it, especially if you haven't attempted a lob in this situation before. It's also a good idea to lob when your opponent is crowding the net too much. He'll have to move back to return your lob. Do not hit a lob that is too high when your opponent is at the net, however, because that gives him time to retrieve it. Hit the lob just a few feet beyond his reach. If you are persistent in lobbing over your opponent's head when he rushes the net, you will not only tire him but also discourage him from coming up to the net again.

It's a good idea to mix lobs with passing shots to keep the net player on his toes and to keep him from crowding the net. The best lob is toward the backhand side. The defensive lob, of course, is used when your opponent is aggressive and is hitting deep shots that you can barely reach. In this case, you should try to hit the ball as high and as deep as possible. This will allow you to recover your balance and equanimity. One of the great masters of the lob is Bobby Riggs, and even in middle age he is able to use this to great psychological advantage, as in his victory over Margaret Court.

If you really want to improve your morale and demoralize your opponent, develop an effective topspin lob. This stroke involves a forward motion of the racket head from under the ball and a follow-through way up and high, almost in a 90-degree path, rolling the racket over the ball at the completion of the shot. The forward rotation makes the ball move faster on the rebound, and it drops quickly after reaching the top of its trajectory. The topspin lob is a difficult shot recommended only for advanced players. This shot is extremely effective when hit correctly and is almost impossible to return. It's an all-or-nothing shot that can demolish an opponent psychologically. It's a good idea to come to the net after a topspin lob because in addition to the advantage of attack, you will be on top of the ball when it is hit back weakly.

OVERHEAD

The overhead, of course, is the coup de grâce of tennis. The overhead smash is the final point of attack and the knockout punch. When you are going to play someone who likes to lob, it is a good idea to practice your overhead. Practicing overhead slams should be part of warming up. Begin by asking your opponent to hit you some short, soft lobs and then some farther back. With expert players, the overhead is used to finish a point concisely. This is the reason that it is wise not to hit an overhead too easily and not to "flub" the shot, because it is very easy to do. Do not always smash the ball to the same spot, or your opponent will anticipate it. Often it is not the hardest hit smash but the one with the best angle that ends the point. It is rather interesting that when you are out of practice the first stroke that lets you down is the overhead, primarily because it requires more precise timing than any other stroke. Obviously the wind will have a great deal to do with the way you hit an overhead, and if you find that your opponent is hitting lobs that swirl around in the wind, it might be a good idea to let them bounce before hitting them. Remember, however, that in the extra time that you now have to hit the ball, a certain amount of anxiety will build up, so take your time in smashing the ball after it bounces.

THE DROP SHOT

The drop shot, like the lob, is a very effective way to break up the rhythm of your opponent's game. It also has the physical effect of tiring your opponent. A good combination is to drop-shot and then to lob your opponent, or to lob first if your opponent is at the net, then drop-shot the next one. These two shots, used in combination, will wear him out. The lob and the drop shot also are the two most devastating shots psychologically. There is nothing more disconcerting to a good player than to race wildly at a little old drop shot and miss it completely. Some people do not like to run, and the more you make them move up and back with drop shots, the more it irritates them. The great advantage of the drop shot is its surprise, so use it sparingly.

The following are some general rules regarding drop shots:

1. Never drop-shot a ball that is hit deep, only a short ball.
2. If you should happen to get a drop shot hit by your opponent when he is not at the net, try to hit another drop shot in return.
3. Do not drop-shot unless your opponent is standing behind the base line.
4. The drop shot is a good weapon against slow runners, players who are out of shape, and players who do not like to come up to the net. It is also an excellent way to draw people to the net, where they are uncomfortable.

Choosing Your Shots

Strategy is just as important in tennis, which is relatively strenuous, as it is in chess, which requires almost no physical exertion. Like chess, tennis demands a game plan. The plan, of course, depends very much on you and your opponent. You should keep in mind some general maxims. First, the shots you *like* to hit may not be the shots you *should* hit. For example, you may be an expert at hitting a drop shot, and your drop shot may feel just great every time you hit it. If you hit this too often, however, it will no longer surprise your opponent, and you will be passed consistently if you hit too many drop shots. You may love to lob and be an expert lobber, but if you play someone who never misses an overhead, it is foolish to feed your opponent his best shot.

The game should also be played in accordance with your own strengths and weaknesses in making shots. If you have a poor backhand, you should avoid this shot whenever you can without getting yourself too far out of position. Even if you do have a weak backhand, you should avoid running around your backhand, since your opponent will hammer you if he knows you'll try to run around it. If you have a weak volley, avoid rushing the net. The same goes for your opponent. If you note that your opponent has a tendency to hit his backhand down the line, then when you do hit your return to his backhand, step toward that line before he swings. If you notice that your opponent always hits his forehand cross-court, move over to that line. If he has a short second serve, move in on his serve for the kill. If he has difficulty moving to one side or the other, try lobbing to the side where he has difficulty moving.

You must decide whether to play strength versus strength or weakness versus weakness. Usually one side is stronger than the other. In general, if you and your opponent both have good forehands, analyze whose forehand will withstand the pressure better. If your opponent's strong side is better than yours, then try playing your weaker side to his weaker side. Your weaker side may be stronger than his. In this case playing your weakness against his would be the best strategy. Remember that you are only as good as your weakest shot.

Some players have trouble with topspin; some hate to return a slice or a chop. You should try out these shots to see whether they bother your opponent. Some players like high-bouncing balls, so in this case minimize your topspin.

On the other hand, some players prefer low slice shots so they can hit over the ball. In this case, try not to slice so much by flattening out your stroke or hitting overspin. Under no circumstances should you give your opponent his favorite shot. Use the shot that will cause him the most trouble.

Actually, court strategy involves not only having a general plan or pattern but also hitting the right shots at the right time. It is obviously impossible to explain what to do in all situations in tennis, but let's look at some situations and discuss what to do in them. In any situation, there is a "hitter" who serves and a "receiver" who receives the service. Let's assume that there is a rally, and the hitter hits the ball to the receiver near the service line. Usually the receiver will hit the ball back near the hitter's service line. At this point the hitter will return the ball about a yard or two in front of the receiver's base line, thus allowing the receiver to continue forward and possibly pass the hitter. However, if the hitter does not send the ball deep and instead slices sharply—a chip shot—then the ball will die sharply. The receiver will have difficulty returning the ball since at this point he has to rush in and dig the ball up from a low position near the middle of the service line and try to pass the hitter, who is at the net. The point is that the hitter used an element of psychological surprise in chipping the shot instead of slamming it to the base line.

After the Serve

Another general tactical procedure that is probably more technical and strategic than psychological is what to do immediately after serving. Almost all top players come to the net on their first service and invariably on their second serve. If you do not come up far enough after serving, how-

ever, you will find yourself "hung up" in what tennis players call "no man's land"—that is, in a spot where your opponent can either pass you or hit the ball at your feet with
or without a bounce, making it extremely difficult for you
to return it. Thus, it is an axiom when serving to come all
the way up to the net or stay back completely.

You should remember that the lines on a tennis court,
like the squares on a chessboard, do not move; only you and
your opponent do. You should know these lines and think
of them as positions on a chessboard and learn the geome-
try of the court. Just as in serving and coming to the net,
there are certain strategic and psychological steps to take in
defending against the net rusher. As you know, people very
often do not come up to the net immediately after their
serve. If you see that your opponent is the slightest bit hesi-
tant in coming to the net after his serve, instead of trying
to pass him with a hard shot down the line, hit a soft one
at his feet, if possible at the service line, and trap him. Make
certain, however, that your opponent is not at the net when
you hit this soft shot, because such a shot can be pulverized
by an adept net player when he is at the net.

In general, the more your opponent crowds the net,
the more you will want to hit down the line. On the other
hand, however, when your opponent is rushing the net, short
angle shots are just as effective, since he is coming toward
you in a straight line. It is not necessarily true that the best
passing shot is a hard one. Most players feel rushed when
their opponent charges the net, so they end up rushing themselves when they try to hit a passing shot. Never let your
opponent rush you and keep you from maintaining your
rhythm. Always take your time when hitting a passing shot.
A change of pace will catch your opponent off guard. When
your opponent is tired and comes to the net, lob!

The Backcourt

Thus far we have discussed strategy in connection with three situations—the serve, coming to the net, and defending against the net man. We will now discuss strategy in the backcourt game. In this game, one of the primary strategies is to try to make your opponent cover as much ground as possible. The best way to do this is to play him from side to side, although it is not axiomatic that these shots be alternated strictly in rotation. The element of surprise is paramount in all phases of tennis, including the backcourt. Thus, when you are alternating from side to side, it is wise after the third or fourth alternation to hit the ball to the same side as the previous shot and maybe catch your opponent off guard.

A second pattern strategy is to hit the balls alternately deep and short. This pattern is difficult to break once it has been established. You should hit the third or fourth shot to the same side as the previous one. In general in backcourt exchanges, hit the ball cross-court. By using this pattern, you get more angle and more court to which to hit. When returning a serve to a net rusher, aim for the down-the-line return. Strive for flexibility, and try to prevent your opponent from learning to anticipate your moves.

In long backcourt rallies, it is a good idea to let your opponent dictate the pattern. If you are well grooved in a pattern, don't change it unless you have drawn your opponent clearly to one side of the court. It is important that you hit the shot well, however. For example, in a cross-court backhand exchange going back and forth many times, it is simpler and easier to hit every backhand than it is to initiate a change down the line. However, if you see that your opponent is sliding all the way over toward his backhand side, surprise him with a down-the-line shot. Just be sure you hit it well, or you may set him up for a forehand cross-court winner.

As indicated before, it's always important to keep your eye on the ball and know instinctively the layout of the court. The average player, however, often mistakenly rivets his eyes on his opponent, watching him as he flits around. This is a mistake. Although you should have a good "feel" for where your opponent is, the main rule in tennis is to keep your eye on the ball. Watching your opponent is secondary.

chapter four

Doubles

Vincent Richards, one of the great doubles players of all time, had this to say, "Nothing is more spectacular than a first-class doubles match; even more than singles play, the doubles game provides a test of generalship and resourcefulness that challenges the utmost concentration and ingenuity of the player."

Jack Kramer said,

In commenting on the qualifications for the ideal doubles player, I would like to emphasize a factor which is all too often overlooked. Others have pointed out the importance of various strokes, maintaining the offensive, etc. I want to stress anticipation. The thing which separates the great from the near-great doubles players is the uncanny ability to anticipate the actions of their opponents. This art is not well understood by the average doubles player, especially the youngsters.

But it is something which can and should be developed through thought and practice.

There are four parts to anticipation. The first is in the placing of your own shot. Suppose you and your partner are at the net and your opponents have one man at net, and one on his way in to net. You hit a volley near the middle of the court that bounces at the service line, so that the advancing opponent must get set to play a ground stroke from that point. By placing your volley there you have taken the first step in anticipating the return because you should know what to look for. In this instance you should look for one of three types of returns—a drive down the center, a dink at your feet, or a well-hidden lob hit over the longest dimension of the court.

The second is in developing knowledge of the method of stroking and types of strokes most used by the opponent about to strike the ball. This involves learning the give-away motions of stroke production, idiosyncrasies, habits, and favorite shots of the opponents under certain tactical conditions.

The third is in concentrating on the motions of the opponent as he is in the act of striking the ball. You should watch the position of his feet, body, arm, backswing, and racquet. These details may appear to be complicated, but after practice they can be noted at a glance. In this way you can detect which one of the three shots he intends to make.

The fourth and final thing is for you and your partner to shift position to meet the by-now well-anticipated return. This move can not be started too soon as it might permit the opponent to change his mind.

Yes sir, give me a partner with the "feel" of anticipation and he will have made a long stride toward being the dream doubles player.[1]

The game of doubles probably has more psychological implications than the game of singles, primarily because there are four people involved—two on each side—resulting in all sorts of psychological interplay. The first important step in doubles is picking a partner. Partners should complement (not necessarily compliment) each other. The choice of a partner should be made not only on the basis of technical ability but also on how well you get along with your potential partner. You should remember that there are all kinds of stresses and strains that come up during the course of a doubles match, and there is always a tendency to blame the other person when your side loses a point. If this becomes chronic, severe friction may arise between partners, resulting in a complete disruption of the game. Thus, if one of the partners has an explosive personality and is easily angered, the other partner should be a calm person. A good example of this was the Davis Cup team of Dennis Ralston and Chuck McKinley. Ralston was prone to temperamental outbursts, particularly because of his own tennis foibles. Every time Ralston would make what he thought was a poor shot, McKinley would come up and calm Ralston and prevent what could have been a disastrous argument. In some instances, each partner settles the other. An example close to home is Cecilia Martinez. For many years her partner was Esme Emanuel, the great South African player. Each was a settling influence in the successful team of Martinez and Emanuel.

In picking a partner, you should respect his or her

---

[1]William Talbert and Bruce Old, *The Games of Doubles in Tennis* (New York: Holt, 1956), pp. 52–53.

abilities. If you have such respect, you will be less likely to blame when something goes wrong. It does not always follow that two great singles players make a good doubles team. It may be that both are heavily individualistic and not prone to cooperate. There is a certain doubles sense that many good singles players lack. In fact, two mediocre singles players may possibly combine to form a good team if they coordinate well and develop a good sense of doubles strategy.

The only way to find out if someone plays doubles well is to observe him or her with others and to play with the person yourself. Some players combine well with just about anyone, but others only play well in doubles with a good partner. Sometimes the partnership clicks immediately. More often than not, however, it takes a while to develop a sense of solidarity and confidence in the partnership.

If you do find a partner who fits your personality, hopefully he has approximately the same ability as you. If you pick someone considerably better and he agrees to play, it may enhance your game so that you play "over your head." However, what usually happens is that you ultimately put too much pressure on yourself and blame yourself every time you lose. Likewise, if your opponents realize that you are considerably weaker than your partner, they will feed everything to you. You will tire, and you will naturally begin to make more than your share of errors. Your partner may try to help you by poaching. If he poaches, or invades your territory, too often, it leaves half the court open for the other team. Then, although your partner may encourage you outwardly, and though he may try hard to be nice to you, he may have second thoughts about playing with you again.

Playing with a partner who is much better than you are can be a very frustrating experience. If your partner is understanding and sympathetic, he may relieve your anxiety, but if he is not, you may have a miserable time.

Sometimes a good player will ask a player of lesser ability to play because other players are not available at the time. In this case, the good player is settling for less, so usually he will try to make the best of the situation and not try to pressure his partner. On the contrary, he will try to be helpful and offer suggestions to improve the partnership. The partner will be nervous, and the better player should be sensitive to this. It is not a good idea to play with a partner who gives you a hard time. It will inevitably hamper your play, and you may unconsciously want to lose just to get even. If you do not get along with your partner off the court, you may also unconsciously try not to win. It is important to find a partner you can get along with both off and on the court.

It is probably best to play with the same partner all the time. A good team, no matter what their difficulties, will inevitably improve with experience. There will be some good and some bad results. On completion of a match, the partners should discuss why and how they won or lost the games in which they played. Open communication is essential for improving and maintaining a partnership. It is important, especially in championship play, to spend some time together discussing strategy. It is a good idea to talk things over before and after playing matches to consolidate your strategy and enhance your rapport and morale.

Likewise it is important to communicate on the court. Some players do not like to talk to or even look at their partners for fear of losing concentration. Lack of communication is all right if things are working well, but if they are not, then it is wise for the partners to have a huddle and discuss what is happening. Perhaps one partner is poaching too much but not putting the ball away. Maybe one partner is missing all his or her first serves, and the second serve is so weak that the net man becomes a target at which to shoot. Perhaps one partner is blasting every return instead of occasionally changing pace by lobbing or dinking returns of serve. These and other possibilities may make it imperative that the partners take stock of the situation.

After you have played with one partner for a while, it becomes easy to sense when your partner is discontented with your play, even if he or she does not actually tell you. His mannerisms will convey the nonverbal message. It is important to discuss your partnership after the match is over. But never decide at that time to tell your partner that this is the last match you'll be playing together.

Some players have difficulty keeping a partner. Frequently they do not get along with their partner for reasons such as these:

1. They insist on taking balls that aren't theirs.
2. They poach and leave the court wide open without putting the ball away.
3. They continually blame the other partner if they are losing.
4. They always tell the other partner what to do when the partner is making all the errors, or they never listen to what the other partner has to say.
5. They give up when the partnership is losing.
6. They insist on serving first all the time even with a poor serve.
7. They take all the credit for winning.
8. They get upset when the other partner misses a shot.
9. They never encourage the other partner.

There should be a certain amount of "forgive and forget" in doubles partnerships; doubles always involves forgetting the flubs—the very poor shots that your partner is apt to make. Actually, doubles has all sorts of connotations insofar as partners are concerned. Doubles partners can be unrelated people (two men, two women, or a man and a woman), or they can involve family relationships. Doubles that pair up family members are becoming increasingly popular in tournaments: father-son, mother-daughter, mother-son, father-daughter, husband-wife, brother-sister, brother-brother, sister-sister, and so on. Each of these has its own set of psychological variables, and on the court, family members tend to behave toward one another the same way they behave toward each other off the court. For example, if a husband and wife have a tendency to argue and fight, this tendency will only be accentuated by the stresses and strains on the court. On any given weekend in tennis clubs throughout the country, you can see the wrangling of husband-wife doubles teams. This is true *only* of married couples who have difficulty off the court. We do not recommend husband-wife doubles as therapy for couples who have marital problems; very often additional problems arise because of the tennis.

Once a partnership has been formed, and you think you can "live" together and are compatible as a team, you and your partner should make additional efforts to encourage one another by voice, action, and attitude. This should take place not only when your partner hits a good shot, but especially when he or she hits a bad one. Encourage your partner by saying that his next shot will undoubtedly be good.

In all doubles, you should employ certain basic stratagems regardless of the partner you have. First, in contrast to singles, doubles is primarily a net game and thus relies heavily on good volleying. When you serve, do so to the backhand down the middle from the right court; from the left court, serve near the side line, not near the center line as in singles. When your partner is serving, concentrate on protecting the center line, not the side line. Thus, since the overwhelming majority of points are won at the net, the primary objective in doubles is to rush the net. This should be an aggressive method of attack and not a defense.

Second, in contrast to singles, the position of being at the net—not power from the backcourt—is foremost. Standing in the correct place for service is also very important. You should note where *each* of your opponents usually serves and position yourself in the proper spot for each serve. What usually happens is that the average player stands in the same spot against all servers. Unlike in singles, you should not try to return the service with a deep drive to the base line, because it can be intercepted easily by the net men. If possible, the return service should be a shallow cross-court shot. In returning second serves, do not try to murder the ball, for the same reason that you should not try to hit the first return of service hard; it will give the net man a waist-high ball to angle back at the side lines.

The game of doubles is different because you have another person to associate with on your side and you must do certain things when he or she is in certain positions. For example, when your partner is receiving the serve, you should edge up just inside your service line, and after you see what happens when he returns the ball, either come to the net if the return is strong or hustle back to the defensive on the base line if his return is weak.

There is always the question of poaching, or encroaching upon your partner's side to cut off a shot. You should not be afraid to poach when your partner is receiving, since you will not have to run so far for a shot. It might be a good idea at times to feint poaching in an attempt to throw your opponents off and worry them. When your partner is serving, the usual place to stand is in the center of the service court about halfway between the net and the service line. Do not become nervous or edge towards the alley, because there is a wide open space there; try to stay toward the middle where the action is.

It is best that both players either stay up at net or both stay back. It is not wise to maintain what is known in tennis circles as a "one up and one back" formation, because it creates a weak and unconsolidated team. The best offensive position is for both players to be at the net, and the best defensive position for both to be on the base line (photo 7). A good offense is always preferable to a defense and will win almost all the time.

A good doubles player can play either forehand or backhand court, but usually he or she will specialize on

PHOTO 7. *In doubles the best offensive position is for both players to be at the net; the best defensive position is for both to be at the base line.* (Photo, *Russell Adams.*)

one side. It is usually better to play the same half of the court with the same partner. When playing with a new partner, you should try finding a backhand player if you specialize in the forehand court, and vice versa. In order to determine your compatibility, you and your partner should each play one set on each side to determine what the best positions are for both. In the case of doubles with one left-handed partner, there may be an advantage in his taking wide shots meant for the right-hander's backhand. The disadvantage in this arrangement, however, is that it creates a weak "middle two backhands." If the left-hander plays the forehand court, it creates a strong center but encourages forehand clashes. Then the shot must be hit by the player who has the stronger forehand, which leaves the wide angles more vulnerable. In general, however, a strong center is more important, because it is there that more balls are hit and played.

The Australians have devised a devilish maneuver known as the "drift." Its purpose is to take advantage of a dink or cross-court return of service by the receiver. The partner of the receiver, when noticing that the receiver is making an effective return of service (either dinking or cross-courting), leaves his regular position and makes a "semi-poach" on the side of the partner. He thus is in position to put away a weak volley by the server or force the server to volley wide. Another tactic developed by the Australians is "packing the center." When the two doubles partners are at the net, they position themselves so that they are closer to each other than to either outside alley line. Most volleys are hit toward the center of the court, where the net is lower and the chances of hitting out are less, so the partners have a favored strategic position.

One tactical maneuver in doubles that is not used in singles is signaling, akin to the signaling of coaches in baseball, but done by the players. Signaling is used extensively in poaching. Before the server makes his delivery, the net man turns and faces the base line so that the opponents cannot see the signal. Very often the concentration of the opponents is broken by the very fact of signaling.

As with singles, you should know some strategic and psychological principles of the various shots in doubles.

THE DOUBLES SERVE

The serve in doubles is undoubtedly the most important shot, and Fred Perry says that possession of a strong serve is even more important in doubles than in singles. The successful serve in doubles not only puts the ball in play but also enables the server to come to the net, putting the serving team in a commanding position. The most important single objective in serving is to put the *first* service into play. Top teams successfully deliver about 80 per cent of their first serves, and approximately 20 percent of winners result from first serves, while only 1 percent result from second serves. Although control of the serve is very important in singles, it is superimportant in doubles.

The objective of a well-placed, controlled serve is to force a defensive return. In general, the first serve should be to the backhand and deep in the service court—to allow the server to come safely in to the net. This serve is best because it is usually hit with three-quarters speed and thus allows the server ample time to come to the net. Some people think that the hard cannonball serve is more effective in doubles. However, this serve, although sometimes forcing a defensive return, is difficult to control and cuts down on the time the server has to get to the net. The cannonball sometimes throws the server off balance and causes him to expend a great deal of energy.

Tactics in doubles, as in singles, are very important

insofar as the service is concerned. Surprise is just as valuable. For example, in doubles, if the server notices that the receiver tends to move in and run around the second serve to slam the ball with his forehand, he can catch the receiver off balance by slicing the second serve to the forehand corner.

As stated before, teamwork is essential in doubles, and its importance begins to show immediately after the ball is put in play. The net man on the server's side should watch the serve, but immediately after it lands, he must shift his attention from the server to the receiver. At this point he must try to anticipate the receiver's stroke from a variety of clues—the receiver's stance, the way in which he prepares to make his stroke, where the return will go, and so on. At this point psychology can make a difference. The net man should not move until the receiver has committed his shot—except in the case of a "fake." A premature start in any direction leaves the serving team open for a placement. Thus, the net man, although he may fully anticipate the shot of the receiver, must conceal this anticipation until the receiver has actually struck the ball. The receiver also has a split second between the striking of the ball in the service box and his swing to alter the direction in which he originally thought he would hit. The importance of the net man or woman in doubles can be seen readily. He must position himself according to his anticipation of the receiver's shot. By noting the eyes, feet, and stance of the receiver, the net man can anticipate the return—a lob, an alley shot, a cross-court, or a straight return.

RETURN OF SERVE

The return of a serve is considered by many to be the most important shot in doubles—even more important than the serve itself. The reasoning is that if you win all your serves, you still must win your opponent's serve at least once to win a set. All successful doubles players have a good and consistent return of serve. They can be counted on to keep the ball in play, especially on crucial points. They have a good sense of what kind of return to make. They rarely try to pass the net man down the alley except occasionally to "keep him honest." The objective of the return of serve in doubles is to enable the receiving team to take the offensive and the net. Time is of the essence. After the delivery of the serve, every second favors the server, since it permits the serving team to gain the net. Thus, after noting where the server usually hits both his first and second serves, the receiver should try to get the ball on the rise, immediately after it comes off the ground. In addition to other advantages, this will obviate the advantage of the peculiar bounce of the American twist and not pull the receiver out of position. By taking the ball on the rise, the doubles receiver gives the server little time to come all the way to the net. The receiver may also have a chance to come up to the net himself, thus creating an offensive position out of a defensive one.

A maneuver that often upsets a server in doubles is rolling with the serve. Rolling is a maneuver by the receiver to run around while the ball is thrown up by the server. This will catch the eye of the server and cause him to hurry or try to change the direction of the serve.

One mistake that many clubplayers make is running around the backhand. Running around serves hit into the backhand corner puts the receiver out of position and opens the court to the opponent's first rally.

The following are different kinds of returns of serves:
1. Dink
2. Severe topspin stroke
3. Flat drive hit cross-court

4. Slice

5. Lob

Variety and surprise are the two psychological variables that are important in the receiver's game. The receiver should be able to hide his intentions until the last second and, depending on the actions of the serving team, be able to return using any of the listed shots. The serving team should not be able to anticipate what the receiver will do. The receiver must mask and vary his return of service, but he also must keep one eye on the net man's movements while executing the return.

NET PLAY

Net play is extremely important in singles but crucial in doubles. About 37 percent of all strokes and 55 percent of winning shots are made from the net in doubles. Split-second timing and uncanny anticipation at the net are musts for a winning doubles team. The net player in doubles must be at the right place at the right time. It is essential for him to keep his eye on his partner and have an understanding with him concerning certain kinds of shots so he can cover court width and also know when to duck to allow him to hit shots that he would normally block. Innumerable shots are open to net players: the deep volley, the angle volley, the overhead, soft, or drop volley, the lob volley, the poach, and the drift. One big problem in doubles is which partner should hit a given shot. Only the experience of the partners will determine this, but there are some general rules to follow:

1. On a return of serve down the center, it is the duty of the net man to try to volley it away. However, the server must be prepared to back him up, since sometimes the net man will find he cannot reach the ball or cannot play it effectively.

2. Lobs hit down the middle should be smashed by the person in the backhand court, since his forehand is toward the center of the court.

3. Partners should have some prearranged signals such as "all right," "yours," "mine," and so on. Quite often there is a question as to who should take a ball, and one player may be caught off balance by the surprise tactics of the opponents.

4. A ball hit down the center should be taken by the player with his forehand toward the center unless his partner's backhand is better and more effective. With two right-handed players, this means the player in the backhand court should take the shot.

5. The net man should watch what his partner is doing as soon as his partner advances after making the first volley. The server may have done a variety of things— fallen down, stayed back instead of coming up to the net because he thought his serve was too easy, or dropped his racket. The net man must be ready to respond to any of these occurrences.

Ordinarily there is a division of labor in doubles concerning hitting certain shots. An understanding is gradually developed about who should hit what. For example, one player may be more effective at net than in the backcourt. Thus it would be wiser to keep him at the net when he is lobbed than for him to retrieve the lob. He should let his partner get it so he can remain at the net. If the net man has a good overhead from the backcourt and his partner is better at net, then he should retrieve the lob himself. However, there are special cases. "Percentage" tennis calls for the net man to cross over and let his partner in the backcourt cover the lob. If both partners are at the net and one player is lobbed, the player who is lobbed should retrieve the shot if it is on his side. Varying circumstances and experience of each other's strengths and weaknesses, however, may indicate that partners should use a pattern other than that specified for playing percentages under usual conditions.

Another example of understanding that comes with experience is who should serve first. In tournament play and even in practice, some players are more nervous at the beginning and not as warmed up as others. They may simply need a few games to get into top form. In this case, it would be best for such a player not to serve first. There is a certain psychological advantage in winning your first service game. Thus it is important that the better server or the one who is not nervous serve first. Sometimes the better server is having temporary problems with his serve. Then it might be better to let his partner serve first. In general, however, try to maintain the same pattern of serving throughout every match.

Unless one player is having unusual difficulty winning his serve, it is best to keep serving on the same side. This maintains the serving rhythms of both players. In addition, by staying on the same side, one becomes more familiar with the wind pattern, the position of the sun, and the backdrop of the court.

The elements also determine in part where one or the other partner will serve. One partner may serve better against the wind and/or into the sun than the other partner, and this partner should serve on the unfavorable side. If one player has a weak serve, it can be considerably strengthened by serving with the wind. Thus it is a good idea to work around the conditions of play and use them to each player's advantage.

The Overhead

In usual doubles play, each person takes care of balls hit in his or her direction and usually does not cross over too far to his partner's side, leaving the team out of position. However, on a short lob that comes to the partner's side, the net man may, if he thinks it feasible, smash at a better angle for the placement and may therefore poach.

The hardest overhead is not necessarily the best to hit. A well-angled shot may win the point just as well, but remember it must be well angled or it can easily be returned for a winner. The kind of overhead that gives some players a sense of power is one that goes over the fence after bouncing on the opponent's court. But if you have the choice of hitting an overhead on the fly or with a bounce, hit it on the fly. This rushes your opponents psychologically and gives them less time to prepare for the return. When playing on grass, always hit the ball before it bounces, because on this uneven surface you may get a bad bounce. If the opposing team lobs over both partners' heads, and if the man on the opposite side to where the ball is hit senses where the ball will land, he is permitted to take the lob. Finally, when the sun is at a bad angle for one partner, the other partner may hit the shot even though it's not on his side.

THE SOFT AND STOP VOLLEYS

The purpose of the soft volley is to force a weak return when all four players are at the net. The soft volley may be a desperation defense shot and a low soft volley that lands at the feet of the opponents may catch them off guard and force one of them to hit a weak return for you to kill off. The stop volley is discussed on page 48.

MIXED DOUBLES

Here we will discuss mixed doubles in which the male and female have no blood or marital relationship. Family doubles will be discussed later. Usually mixed doubles teams in tournaments are formed by a male player asking a

female player to play with him. In championship class, this
is usually done strictly on the basis of ability. It is rather
interesting that with certain exceptions, championship mixed
doubles teams tend to change and rarely last for more than
a few years, as doubles teams of the same sex do. This may
be because there are no institutionalized mixed sex competitions in tennis. For example, the Davis Cup and the Wight-
man Cup are strictly unisex competitions. In championship
play, tournament mixed doubles are not as popular in the
United States as they are in Europe.

The way a male treats his female tennis partner is a reflection of the way he treats females in general. Likewise,
a woman may treat her male partner as she treats other men.
If a man is insecure in the presence of females, he will tend
to be overly aggressive with women on the tennis court. If
he has hostility toward women, he will tend to dominate
and be hostile toward his female partner. If he tends to be
protective toward females, he will tend to poach and protect his partner from the terrifying shots of their opponents.
In general an aggressive man on the court will tend to be
more inhibited in exhibiting his aggression with a female
partner than with a male. For example, he may swear at
himself or at his male partner, but will tend to do that less
if his partner is a woman.

In mixed doubles, men may also try to be entertaining
by making wisecracks and jokes more often than they do
when playing with a partner of the same sex. All the people
involved tend to be more polite, using such expressions as
"take two" on questionable second serves, especially when
the server is a woman. Some male players think, insofar as
strategy is concerned, that it is best to hit the ball consistently to the female opponent. This strategy does not always
work, however, since often the female on the other side of
the net is steadier than the male. Very often men make the

mistake of underestimating the ability of the female partner.

A woman, of course, is also affected by having a male partner. She may act flirtatious or coy and let the man take shots that she should have returned herself. Or, if she tends to compete with men, she may try to dominate the play and resent the attempts of her male partner to protect her by returning shots that were rightfully hers..

In general, even outside of championship play, men will make the choice of a partner, but with the advent of Women's Liberation, this proclivity has diminished. The same general principles of psychology and strategy that hold for doubles also hold for mixed doubles. It should be noted that in all the great mixed doubles teams throughout the globe, the female partner has been an outstanding tennis player.

Mixed doubles, like any other kind of doubles, requires a coordinated effort. The man and woman must work together to complement each other. The best mixed doubles team will be the most equally balanced one. The better player (who usually is the man) should dominate the team and take as many shots as possible. However, a man should not take shots that are set-ups for his female partner. He should let her play all the shots on her side. If the ball is in the middle, he should take it. Very often, however, males underestimate the ability of their female partners, or psychologically they feel they must dominate the play. If the woman is better, *she* should be the dominant player. Usually the man takes the backhand court, but this may be reversed if the woman has a better backhand than the male. (In the team of Rosemary Casals and Ilie Nastase, Ms. Casals usually played the backhand court.)

In occasional situations, such as a consolation round in which partners are assigned, a partner may play with someone against his will. The "assigned" partner may be inferior to one the player would ordinarily choose. In such a situation, even if your assigned partner is hopeless, you should maintain your equanimity and not lose your temper even when the assigned player misses easy shots. Remember that there will be other tournaments, and tournament officials will take into account your behavior at previous times.

HUSBAND-WIFE TEAMS

Some psychological implications of husband-wife doubles have been mentioned previously. However, husbands and wives *can* win championships. There have been nine husband-and-wife teams that have won national championships in the United States and other countries. The only husband-wife team to win United States Lawn Tennis Association (USLTA) mixed doubles grass championship was Mr. and Mrs. Clarence Hobari, in 1905. In 1926, Mr. and Mrs. Leslie A. Godfrey won two mixed doubles championships at Wimbleton; they were the only ones to do this. The first married couple to win the Canadian mixed doubles was Mr. and Mrs. Wilmer Allison in 1938. Mr. and Mrs. Morey Lewis won in 1946, and Mr. and Mrs. Robert J. Kelleher in 1947. The Kellehers also won the USLTA Hard-Court mixed doubles in 1958, 1960, and 1964. Mr. and Mrs. Elwood Cooke won the USLTA Clay-Court title in 1945. In Australia, Mr. and Mrs. Harry Hopman won the Australian mixed doubles championships in 1936, 1937, and 1939.

There is really no behavioral rule of thumb insofar as husband-and-wife doubles teams are concerned. In general, the husband is less tolerant—at least overtly—of bad shots made by his wife then he would be of those made by another female partner. He usually has more of a tendency to give advice (which usually is not taken) to his wife on the court in cases where the reverse is true off the court—possibly a mechanism for getting back for abuse he receives at home. Occasionally, disputes will arise after the match over the way the husband viewed the female opponent and vice versa. If you see that you and your spouse do not get along on the court, it might be a good idea to split up when playing mixed doubles against another team and prevent the continuation of court conflict at home.

WOMEN'S DOUBLES

The same principles of strategy that apply to men's doubles apply to women's. With the coming of age of women's tennis insofar as prize money is concerned (women's prize money has increased 500 percent), women's tennis has been catching up with men's. An interesting survey was done by the two authors of this book and Esme Emanuel regarding how a select audience views women's as compared with men's tennis. An article describing the survey is given as Appendix C.

FATHER-SON DOUBLES

Father-son doubles are becoming ever more popular in tennis, and national and sectional rankings now are made in this division throughout the country. In many instances in tournaments and in championship class, the father, the son, or both are or have been nationally or sectionally ranked players. Good examples are F. A. Froehling, Jr., and F. A. Froehling, III; H. William Bond and William Bond; Dennis Ralston (who is teamed with his father, Robert Ralston), and so on.

Several anomalous psychological situations may exist in father-son combinations. In practically every other family situation, the father is considered to be the authority figure. In tennis, however, if the son is the better player, the roles may be reversed and the son may be the one to give orders and advice to the father. How the father will react to this will depend on a number of contingencies, the primary ones being how much frustration tolerance the father has and how much he believes in the ability and knowledge of the son in the area of tennis. The father always has a natural tendency to take over the situation, especially in crises, and at those times he can be of value to the team and a stabilizing influence. The son, if he is a better or top tennis player, can take charge of the shots and strategy during the course of the match. Where a difference of opinion and a clash occur on the court, the family members are likely to "replay" the whole match that evening over the dinner table. The father, as the head of the family, may exert his authority and tell the son in no uncertain terms what he thought of his offspring's tennis. The son, instead of giving in to the natural tendency to argue back, should rather take his father's constructive points and combine them with his own analysis to build a sound strategy for subsequent matches.

MOTHER-SON TEAMS

Mother-son teams are less frequent than father-son doubles in tennis, but occasionally this combination is included in some tournaments. We are not suggesting that the Oedipal situation is in full display on the tennis court, but some psychological interplay can be seen in this relationship. For example, there is usually little or no belligerence or anger on the part of the son when his mother misses an easy shot, unlike when his partner is his father. Rather, he tends to show a kind of kindly, protective benevolence: "You can do better, Mom—and I'm sure next time you will."

MOTHER-DAUGHTER DOUBLES

The same behavioral circumstances that apply to mother-son doubles apply to a limited extent in mother-daughter doubles. In mother-daughter doubles, there is sometimes a carry-over of the relations that the team members have outside the tennis court. If mother and daughter have an authority problem at home, the same problem will come up during crucial points in the match. In general, in mother-daughter tennis relationships, the daughter will not show the consideration for her mother that the son will. Much will depend, however, on the personalities of the individuals involved and the entire relationship between the mother and daughter.

FATHER-DAUGHTER DOUBLES

In father-daughter doubles, often a reverse of the relationship between mother and son occurs. Occasionally the Electra complex asserts itself—that is, the affectionate relationship between father and daughter will take over during a match.

SIBLING DOUBLES

Brother-brother, sister-sister, and brother-sister combinations are all sibling teams. There have been relatively few champion sibling teams, although brothers and sisters in the same family sometimes have been outstanding singles players. For example, the McKinley brothers have been nationally ranked tennis players, although at different times. Whitney Reed, ranked number one in the United States in 1942, has a younger sister who is one of the better players in Northern California. Virginia Wolfenden Kovacs Edwards, who was a nationally ranked player, has a younger sister who was a ranked player in Northern California. Chris and Jeanne Evert are nationally ranked players, and Sandy Mayer has a younger brother who is nationally ranked in his age group. None of these siblings, however, have played consistently together as tournament doubles teams. Exceptions to the tournament sibling teams are Joy and

Jill Schwikert (photo 8) and Vijay and Amand Amritraj, the great Indian players, who have competed successfully in international tennis tournaments. In the past Howard and Robert Kinsey and Reginald and Hugh Doherty were outstanding and nationally ranked doubles players.

PHOTO 8.   *Although there have been few champion sibling teams, the Schwikert twins are an exception.*

In the sibling team, whether brother-brother, sister-sister or brother-sister, the usual off-court behavioral characteristics operate during the tennis game. No matter what the tennis ability of the individual players, it is usually the older of the siblings who will lead and dominate the team, just as he does in the family, although there will be exceptions. Sibling rivalry, if there is any, will again come out in a crucial point, and, like husbands and wives who do not get along off the court, siblings who have difficulty in the family should not be doubles partners.

chapter five

The Professional
Tennis Circuit

This chapter will be devoted to a topic that is not strictly in the domain of tennis psychology but is usually not included in books on tennis. The tremendous growth in popularity of tennis has brought with it a concurrent growth of tennis tournaments, tours, and exhibitions. The public is now exposed to a variety of tennis groups, leagues, tournaments, and so on, each with its own bewildering array of subgroups. The sport has changed greatly in recent years, partly because of the advent of Women's Lib. Now there are several women's professional groups on a par with men's groups touring the country and the world. The information contained in this chapter is primarily from the experiences of the female author of this book. It gives an inside glimpse of professional tennis in the Virginia Slims tour but applies to other women's and men's tours as well.

Individuals may be interested in learning how a tennis player can join and play in a particular tennis circuit like World Championship Tennis (WCT), Virginia Slims, or USTA. WCT is an all-male organization sponsored by H. L. Hunt, the Texas millionaire. As of 1975, World Championship Tennis has three groups of players, A, B, and C. The best players are invited to join and compete for top prize money.

In 1974 also, for the first time in three years, the women professionals were together throughout the entire year. (A former split between the USTA and the Virginia Slims group has been mended.) Instead of two circuits, there will now be only one to accommodate all the players. The professionals are not provided transportation, and they do not have guarantees, but they are often provided with housing.

The selection of the best players usually is made according to some arbitrary ranking list based on one's national and international tournament record, national ranking, and past reputation as a player. Local tennis players must qualify in preliminary rounds and are usually allowed to participate and compete for a few openings in the draw.

Some championship professional players do not join an organized tour because they prefer to remain independent and choose where and when they want to play. Once a person commits himself (or herself), he or she is obligated to play a prescribed minimum number of tournaments with that organization. The player loses a certain amount of independence in exchange for security. By joining a tour, he is assured of competing against the very best professionals for prize money.

Gladys Heldman of Houston, Texas—a former nationally ranked player and mother of Julie Heldman, a leading woman professional—was the tour organizer for the Virginia Slims circuit from 1970 to 1973, until the USTA and Women's Tennis Association (WTA) assumed her responsibilities in 1974. She planned and arranged the year-long professional women's tennis circuit and drew up the contracts of the women professionals, the tournament promoters, and often the sponsors.

Mrs. Heldman has said, "Take eight girls, add a dash of Virginia Slims, sprinkle with $7,500, and you have a tasty tennis tournament. To serve in large quantities, increase the mixture to sixty-eight girls, spice with large quantities of Virginia Slims, pour in $880,000, season with British Motors Corporation, Barnett Bank, Max Pax, and Four Roses, and stir for several months. This will feed at least 25,000 spectators a week."

Initially there are three sets of essential people in the organization of a professional tennis circuit—the tour organizer, the promoter or promoters, and the sponsor or sponsors. A tour organizer must first sign up all the players who agree to play the entire circuit. He assures the promoters that only top players will participate. In this way, advance publicity is used to increase the advance ticket sales. The organizer then finds local promoters who are willing to run the risk of putting up money and staging the event in the cities that want to host tournaments. The organizer coordinates the whole circuit and draws up a schedule.

Next, the tour organizer often seeks out sponsors who are willing to advance funds, ordinarily at least half the total needed. The promoter contacts various national companies and business concerns that advertise heavily and might sponsor one or two tournaments.

The overall sponsor for the 1973 Virginia Slims Women's Professional tennis circuit was of course Virginia Slims cigarettes. At times the cigarette company would sponsor a tournament individually and call it a Virginia Slims Invitational. At other times, the promoter or tour organizer obtained another sponsor. Virginia Slims cigarettes would then advance 5 percent of the total prize money, which was turned over to the local promoter in exchange for designating the tournament as a stop on the Virginia Slims circuit.

In return for an advance, the sponsor is guaranteed that his name will be promoted along with the tournament. It becomes, for example, the British Motors Corporation Women's Pro Tennis Championship of San Francisco, or the Max Pax Classic of Philadelphia.

Quite naturally, sponsors are eager to get good publicity for their company. They use tournaments as promotional tools for selling their products, and the tournament may bring many of their potential customers together. Sometimes the president or an important official in the business is a tennis buff, and he may decide to sponsor a tournament. He may enjoy being around tennis celebrities and telling his friends and business associates about his close contact with them.

The local promoter is the one who takes the risks, does all the work, and makes a profit or takes a loss. He has the job of creating the event and putting it together. He determines the location, and he is responsible for selling tickets and doing advance publicity. The promoter rents an auditorium for the week or persuades a private club to hold the tournament. Many new private clubs enjoy the prestige and publicity of having a professional tennis tournament. Older, more established clubs are usually unwilling to donate their facilities because they don't feel they have anything to gain from it. Many members become resentful when their routine is disrupted and they must share club facilities with professionals for a week or more.

Tennis tournaments usually require the addition of bleachers, special concession stands, and supplementary toilet facilities. If the tournament is played indoors, the lighting must be checked to be sure it meets certain minimum standards. If the tournament is played outdoors, rain insurance must be obtained in case the event gets washed out.

The promoter risks the possibility of losing money if the tournament is unsuccessful, but he also makes a profit if everything goes well. There is a great deal of uncertainty involved in promoting tennis tournaments. The promoter may work for six months advancing his tournament, yet he reaps most of his profits only on its last two rounds. He hopes that the top players will appear and won't lose to lesser players in the first few days. He also keeps his fingers crossed about the weather!

Playing on indoor courts is not so much affected by bad weather, but if there is a heavy thunder shower or snowfall, people will be inclined to stay home that day unless they hold advance tickets. The advance ticket sales are a good indicator of how successful a tournament will be. Usually an equal number are sold at the door as are sold in advance.

The promoter also is responsible for getting a sponsor unless the tour organizer has already done so. The promoter tries to sell the value of the tennis tournament to a potential sponsor, hoping to persuade him to pay for the publicity and to put up at least 50 percent of the prize money. The promoter has to advance the remainder.

The promoter may keep the entire gate receipts, but this varies from tournament to tournament. Different contracts are drawn at different locations. Some sponsors advance most of the prize money (which may vary from $100 for first-round winners to $30,000 or more for the tournament winner); some just underwrite the events; and some not only underwrite tornaments but also share in the profits.

The actual staging of the tournament may be done by the sponsor alone or may be delegated. Unless he is running a small organization, he will delegate responsibilities to various tournament officials and committees. The promoter coordinates the activities necessary for running the tournament, but he leaves the details to the tournament chairman.

Volunteers may help save money and effort, even though they may not be as efficient as paid help. Larry King, who used to promote several tournaments on the Women's Pro tour and husband of Billie Jean King, said that he much preferred *hiring* linemen, because then he never had to feel bad about firing them for doing a poor job!

The following personnel connected with tournaments are usually volunteers—director, official referee, umpires, linesmen, ball boys and ball girls, and people responsible for hospitality, housing, transportation, entertainment, court maintenance, concessions, programs, and tickets. The promoter cannot rely solely on volunteer help, however, so he must also hire assistants to help promote and advertise the tournament. He also employs salesmen to sell tickets to individuals, groups, and companies.

It usually takes a few years for a tournament to establish itself in a particular city. Preferably it should be held at the same time each year so that people in the area begin to expect the tournament and make it a major social event. The longer a tournament has been held, the more prestigious and important it seems to become. The Wimbleton tournament is a classic example.

Some promoters are connected with private tennis clubs. They want to advertise their club, especially if it is new and they need to recruit new members. Still other promoters like the prestige and publicity they can generate for themselves. They also like tennis and want to promote tennis interest in their area.

The promoter works very actively in stirring up regional interest for his tournament. He is in close contact with the mass media in advertising the tournament.

Several months before a tournament is held, two representatives from local professional groups meet with the local promoters and sponsors. They check out the facilities to be sure that they are adequate. They make plans to assure that banners, posters, scoreboards, tickets, credentials, and so on will be available. They check over other tournament preparations, such as social events, transportation, housing, and meals. Local public relations arrangements are also made at this meeting, and press facilities—typewriters, telephones, and duplicating machines—are furnished.

About a month before the tournament begins, at least one of the top players on the circuit goes to the city for the second phase in the pretournament activities. This second meeting is a press conference, which is usually a luncheon. The local promoter and sponsor invite representatives of newspapers, wire services, radio, TV, and magazines. The players are the stars of the press conference as they promote the upcoming tournament. They play key roles in getting the media involved with the tournament. The promoter and sponsor hope that the enthusiasm of the professionals will infect those who are interviewing them and that the media will devote space and time to the event.

The professionals have an obligation to promote the various tournaments. Every week they are expected to do promotion work—radio and TV appearances, exclusive interviews, store appearances, free tennis clinics, and attendance at various social functions in conjunction with the tournament.

The tour director coordinates the players with the tournament officials, keeps communication flowing, and makes last-minute arrangements. This person personally confers with the tournament chairman and referee concerning anything that has to do with the players, such as scheduling matches and making the draw.

The tour director represents the players. He or she listens to grievances of the players as well as those of tournament committees. The director sees to it that the players are prompt for their matches and make a good impression. Every week is a different experience for the tour director because he or she deals with different people at each stop. Some tournament officials are very efficient and easy to deal with. Others are not so easy going, and some know absolutely nothing about tennis! Thus the tour director has to be very adaptable and resilient.

The better organized a tournament is, the fewer worries the tour director has. Often, however, unexpected things crop up and it is the tour director's job to smooth things out and try to keep both the players and the promoters happy.

A public relations representative usually travels with the circuit. The biggest responsibility of this person is to make sure that the media cover the tournament adequately. Each week the public relations person arranges for different players to make TV and radio appearances and do magazine and newspaper interviews. He tries to promote the tournament as much as possible by notifying TV stations and news reporters. He makes sure that journalists get the proper credentials to report the tournament and makes arrangements for TV stations to film part of matches for their news coverage. It is important that the media announce and review the tournament; otherwise, very few people are aware that a tournament is taking place. A tournament is held not just for the players but also for the spectators who come and support the tournament. It is the number of paying spectators that determines whether the tournament is successful or not. It is thus critical that the tournament be well publicized and adequately covered.

It is also imperative that the tennis professionals present a positive image of the tour to the media. If people read in the paper of some star's gripes about the tour, they will be inclined to stay home instead of watching the tennis matches the next day. When the professionals present a positive and enthusiastic picture of tennis and the circuit, the enthusiasm will be transmitted to the sportswriters, who in turn will write favorably about tennis in longer and more exclusive stories. Invariably, more people will become aware of and interested in the tournament, and more will come to watch.

Of course, the most important ingredients in a tennis tournament are the players; without them there can be no tournament. But the players cannot survive on their own. They must work very closely with the tournament sponsors, promoters, and officials, because they all need each other in order to have successful tournaments.

Besides actually promoting the tournament and presenting a favorable image to the press, the biggest responsibility of the players is to play well. That is what they do best, and that is what is expected of them. The stage is set for them, and they are expected to perform. They get most of the glory and/or the criticism because they are the stars, the showpieces. People pay to watch them play and compete against one another. And the public is not about to pay for a second-rate performance. They want to see a good show.

Most of the players are extremely aware of their obligation to the spectators. In a sense, they play not only for themselves, but for the audience as well. The greater the number of spectators, the more public and popular the event becomes.

The most popular professionals are not just the winners, but the ones who seem most aware of the spectators and fans. They have a certain rapport with the audience and always give everything they have in order to put on a good performance, win or lose. They are usually cooperative with the press and are willing to sign autographs and chat with their fans. They are the ones who somehow are able to get the spectators emotionally involved in the matches.

As in every group, there are some difficult professionals in tennis who may antagonize the audience and give tournament officials trouble. Fortunately, there are relatively few of these.

Players represent not only themselves. They are "walking billboards" for various sporting goods companies and tennis equipment manufacturers. All professionals on tour get their equipment free—clothes, shoes, rackets, and balls. Representatives from sporting goods companies regularly go to tournaments to be sure that their players are well supplied. They stencil the racket strings so that the initial or trademark of the company will show up better in play.

The clothes and shoes the players wear inevitably advertise the companies that manufacture them. Many spectators are very fashion-conscious and look to the pros to set the fashion trends. It is impossible to avoid the commercial aspect of the game at the professional level. All the top players give endorsements for rackets, shoes, and clothes, and their names become synonymous with the products they are using. The very best pros are paid large sums of money simply to be designated as touring pros of certain prestigious tennis clubs. Often they have to be at the club only one or two weeks a year. They are paid just so their name can be used to add more glamour to the club.

A few professionals also do TV commercials and appear in magazine ads for cars, coffee, deodorants, hair dryers, toothpaste, socks, shampoos, and after-shave lotions. Thus, the more a player promotes himself, the more he will also be indirectly advertising the business concerns with which he is connected. The more successful he becomes, the more distinction his endorsements have.

There are various explanations of why tennis players decide to become professionals. The most obvious reason is to earn a living. What better way is there to make money than by doing what you love to do and what you can do best? For some teaching professionals, playing part-time on the pro tour is good for their business, since it elevates them to a higher status in the eyes of their pupils. If a teaching professional has good results, he will be in greater demand. If he does not do well, the sentiment is, "How can he be expected to beat all the other pros? He is teaching all day while they simply compete in tournaments all year long."

A teaching professional's playing ability is often overestimated by his pupils when he is the best player in the area. Other players are compared to him, and he becomes the standard of perfection. This doesn't happen, though, when there are better players around or when the town is host to an annual professional tournament at which local people have the opportunity to see top pros compete.

A teaching professional who competes in a local tournament feels great pressure to win, especially if the tournament is held at his club. His pupils want him to win because it will elevate his status and consequently theirs. For example, the fact that a teaching pro beat the fifth ranked man or woman in the United States would increase his prestige. His teaching method would be more believable and his ability proven.

Many good teaching professionals, however, are not and need not be top or championship players. They must know the basic techniques and strategy of the game and,

most important, be able to communicate understanding of
tennis to pupils. Fortunately, teaching tennis and playing
tennis are different skills.

Most teaching pros limit themselves to local tournaments, but a few play some major pro tournaments throughout the year. With only a few exceptions, teaching pros
have to struggle just to break even when playing pro tournaments, especially when they have to travel a good deal.
When the pro takes a week off work to play a tournament,
he can label his trip "business expense." It is actually business mixed with pleasure, but it's still tax deductible.

Some young players who join the circuit simply want to
try it out for a couple of years. Playing tennis professionally seems more interesting than getting another kind of
job or going to college. They use the time as an interim
maturation period before deciding on a career. Often these
young people keep on playing and never stop. Other times,
they get a more secure job, such as teaching, or go into
another field related to tennis. Often the young players—
the "rookies" of the tour—are subsidized for a couple of
years before they become financially independent. Parents
or sponsors invest in the possible future success of these
players. The majority never make an impact on the tennis
world, however.

Prize money has increased materially in the last three
years, but it still has a long way to go to be comparable to
other sports such as basketball, football, baseball and even
golf. World Team Tennis (WTT), formed in 1973, should
promote an even greater interest in the game. Originally
there were sixteen franchised teams; as of the writing of
this book the number has been reduced. There are two
geographical divisions, with three men and three women to
a team. There will be a total of ninety-six men and women
contracted to play from May through the middle of August.

There will be men's singles, women's singles, women's doubles, men's doubles, and mixed doubles. The final score is decided on the total number of no-add games won. This way, the outcome of the matches will often be undecided until the termination of the mixed doubles. If the score is tied in the end, then a "super no-add game" is played to decide the match.

First of all, WTT is a team sport. Fans will be able to identify with members of the team. In a tournament, most people usually come to watch just the top players. In team tennis, everyone on the tour is equally important—they are all stars and all share in the excitement and glory. WTT will make tennis comparable with other sports having contracts, guaranteed salaries, regular bonuses, pension plans, and health insurance. The players will also be provided with full-time coaches, trainers, and doctors. They will be free to do anything they want the rest of the year. WTT will be the first major sport in which men and women are in the same positions. By playing mixed doubles, they will be equally responsible for the final scores. Salaries will also be comparable. The top women will earn just as much as the top men. Paid officials will direct the matches. WTT will be relatively easy to promote. Everything will be professionally planned and organized well in advance. Because the fans can know months in advance who will be playing, it will be easier to sell advance tickets. Currently, the top seeded players in a tournament sometimes don't make it through to the final rounds—to the disappointment of fans.

It would be virtually impossible to stay on the circuit for any great length of time if you did not love the game and enjoy playing tennis. The keen demands of competition would eventually take their toll. One must be completely dedicated in order to weather all the disappointments that lie along the road to success.

Definitions of success vary, of course, and success is at least partly a state of mind. One player considers success in terms of simply qualifying for a tournament or winning a few games from a highly ranked player. Another player is not happy unless he wins a tournament or earns more than $100,000 in a year. So success is merely a relative term to describe one's accomplishments, great or small.

All the pros are more or less striving to improve their skills. Some make more demands on themselves than others do. These are the ones who will usually work the hardest and devote themselves completely to the game. They are willing to sacrifice virtually everything in order to perfect their skill. All their energy is narrowed down to becoming better and better tennis players. Their lives are centered around practicing, playing matches, and doing the necessary promotion work for the tournament and for the products they endorse.

The social life of a tennis professional is usually limited to tennis circles. A pro has many opportunities to meet people, but he may have difficulty developing lasting relationships, since he travels ten months of the year. Unless he makes a special effort to see special friends, it becomes hard to sustain interest. There is a constant influx of new faces and opportunities, and the professional often finds himself getting temporarily involved with one person after another in relationships that last only for the duration of one tournament. The pros meet different people every day of their lives, and they often have difficulty remembering the names of everyone they meet. For the fans, however, the tournament is a big social occasion, a glamorous opportunity to meet celebrities. The professionals come into their lives maybe only once a year. Some curious incidents happen. For example, nothing is so disconcerting to a professional as having someone come up and say "Hi! Remember me?" It only serves to embarrass the tennis player unless he can fake it by saying "Sure I do. Yes, now I remember. You look so familiar, but I forgot your name!" Then the person will introduce his children, and the pro tries to remember their names and ages although it was four years ago when he stayed in their house or met them at a cocktail party.

Every tournament has at least one or two social events held in honor of the players—cocktail parties, buffets, or dances. All the people involved with the tournament are invited, especially the patrons, box-seat holders, and committee members. This is an important event for them. Those invited are considered the important people—the "in" crowd of the tennis community. Occasionally the mayor or some other political figure will come. Almost always, the get-together will be photographed and publicized in the social pages of the newspaper the following day, and the top players will be seen posing with several prominent people.

These social gatherings are very important in promoting interest and generating publicity. They enable the tennis crowd to become personally involved with the players, and they serve almost as rewards for the work and time involved in getting a tournament together. They also draw the tennis community together and provide an opportunity for people to establish new contacts involving tennis and business. People can meet both tennis players and other tennis enthusiasts.

Most players understand the promotional value of these social events, but going to so many parties all the time seems to decrease their importance. Parties become routine, and it is easy to lose your enthusiasm, especially when you are asked the same questions every week. The caterers seem to show little imagination in varying their hors d'oeuvres. You are tired from playing hard all day and can barely stand up. Everyone is getting high on cocktails while you stir a glass of soda water and look on.

The tour director puts pressure on all the players, especially the top ones, to attend at least one party a week. The promoters and sponsors must be kept happy, so the players have to make an effort. The lesser players, however, become only added extras because the people are not so much interested in them as they are in meeting the stars. Their absence is not very noticeable.

The stars are always in the limelight. They have to dress well and be polite all the time or they easily become controversial figures. They always have to be careful what they say lest they be misquoted or misinterpreted. There is a lot of pressure on them to present an ideal image. Naturally, they try to fulfill everyone's expectations of how a superstar should act. They are concerned with the fact that they are setting an example to the other players and the public.

The lesser players are not under so much public scrutiny. They have more freedom and privacy, because they don't create as much impact as the stars do. They often become merely supportive actors and actresses in a social situation. The best players are given special consideration in compensation for the pressures that come from being at the top. The others are not given the same royal treatment, but they have more liberty to do and act as they please.

The free hospitality during many tournaments is provided by members of the club, who either volunteer or are pressured by the tournament committee. Most people are deeply honored to have a professional live with them and go to great lengths to make the pro comfortable. They like to show off their guest to their neighbors and take personal pride in his or her achievements. Often they serve formal meals like those they normally reserve for major holidays. They put their best foot forward in an attempt to impress their houseguest. Usually the first few days are quite formal, and then everyone eases up. That is the usual syndrome.

Many players are very receptive to this special treatment and thrive on the attention. The people they stay with become a surrogate family that gives them a sense of security. Others, especially the top pros who can afford it, shy away from private homes and stay in motels or hotels. Taking a lot of time to socialize with their hosts just drains them of much-needed energy, which they want to save for playing tennis. Hotels are impersonal, of course, but they have their advantages—privacy, freedom to come and go, and so on. Hopefully, with the expanded growth of professional tennis, *every* professional tennis player soon will be able to afford his own accommodations.

In a sport like tennis, much of the competition among players is transferred to social situations off the court. The tennis hierarchy, or pecking order, is established according to players' feelings of superiority over certain others. It shows up both on and off the court. Players' relationships can take on the form of "psyching," of establishing the impression that one is better than another. They may play a mental game of "one-upmanship." A person's self-worth becomes determined according to how well he has maintained or improved his position as a player. This is done both subtly and overtly, although it is more effective when one player is unaware of what the other is doing. Here is an example of a hypothetical exchange between two tour players:

PLAYER I: "I've got so much to do tomorrow. First a clinic, then the press conference before I play my match under the lights."

PLAYER II: "Is that all? Last week I had to do two radio

shows, go to a luncheon, and then play two matches that afternoon. I wish they wouldn't keep asking me to do so much, but I guess they really want me.

Another example:

PLAYER I: "How'd you do in your match this morning?"

PLAYER II: "Well I lost to Jim again, this time after having ten match points."

PLAYER I: "You're kidding! How could you lose to him? He hasn't won a match in six months!"

But not all players carry on their rivalries seriously off the court. There is a lot of teasing and joking with a few spurs attached, but it's all considered part of the game. The trick is not to let any of the snide remarks get to you. Either laugh them off, ignore them, or think up even more clever put-downs. The ones who are best able to cope with this rivalry take everything in their stride. They are the ones who also seem to handle themselves better on the court.

Only when a player gets too involved in his self-importance does he become unpopular and isolated from everyone else. On the whole, most players get along quite well and usually make an effort to adjust to one another. The tennis pros on the circuit are such a closely knit group that it is imperative for them to learn how to adapt to the continuous tension of competition. Otherwise the strain would be just too much to live with. Unless one acquires the knack of handling this basic anxiety by using it to his advantage, he will be unable to survive.

In spite of the intense competition, the tennis professionals on tour get to know each other quite well. Because of their close contact, they invariably end up forming lasting friendships with the players who are within the same age and ability level. They travel together, room together, have mutual friends, attend the same social functions, and practice with and compete against each other. Those that join the professional ranks are a heterogeneous group. They come from diverse social, economic, and ethnic backgrounds. They live and play all over the world. Their ages range from about eighteen to over thirty, and their educational backgrounds vary from less than high school to Ph.D's. Tennis is often their only common denominator.

The players on the professional circuit are the best in the world. With the expansion of tennis, the level of play has improved tremendously. The players have had to work themselves up from a local to an international standard of play. They have had to train hard and survive many years of fierce competition. Even after developing the necessary skills, they have had to keep improving and maturing their games.

Surviving on the circuit is extremely demanding, both physically and mentally. It means total involvement for the more ambitious players. On the other hand, pro tennis offers the fringe benefits of international travel, social recognition, and a certain amount of glamour—hard-earned rewards for a difficult and exacting career. The essential thing is that the pro enjoy tennis most of all; otherwise, it hardly seems worth going after its purely monetary rewards. The successful players are the ones who best endure the pressure and heartbreaks of the circuit. They continue with optimism and a sense of purpose in spite of problems. A player's affluence is usually a good indication of his discipline and self-mastery on the court.

Not everyone, however, can be tops. Not everyone has the talent and/or the dedication for pro tennis. Although each player strives to move forward, it isn't feasible for everyone to make it. Each individual decides for himself exactly how much progress and good fortune *he* needs in order to feel that he is a success. Otherwise there can be only *one* success—the number-one pro.

The purpose of this book has been to expose the competitive strategies of tennis, both psychological and technical. Playing tennis is certainly not only a simple athletic contest. It is also a very psychological experience. You can use all the messages and vibrations from your opponents to your advantage or disadvantage. The authors hope that the reader will gain some insight into his own play and that of his rivals, and will experience a significant improvement in his future tennis games.

Rules for Seeding the Draw

All championships and other sanctioned tournaments except handicap events shall have a seeded draw, conducted in accordance with the following rules:

1. (a) The committee in charge of a tournament shall have full power in the making of the draw. In the case of USTA Championships, the committee appointed to represent the USTA shall have such power.

   (b) The number of seeded players shall be determined by the committee, subject to the limitation that not more than 1 player may be seeded for every 4 entries. If a major fraction of 4 entries remains after such procedure, 1 additional player may be seeded.

   (c) The additional seed shall be placed at the top of the first unoccupied group (i.e., half, quarter, eighth, sixteenth, or thirty-second, as the case may be) unoccupied by an American Seed. In the case of a foreign entry it shall be placed at the bottom of such group.

(d) The committee shall rank in order the number of domestic entrants to be seeded according to ability, using as a guide the USTA ranking and sectional rankings of the previous year and the performances of the players during the current year.

(e) When the draw is posted, a list of those players that were seeded and the order in which they were ranked shall be posted also.

2. (a) If two are to be seeded: Numbers 1 and 2 shall be drawn by lot; the first drawn shall be placed at the top of the upper half; the second at the bottom of the lower half.

(b) If four are to be seeded: Numbers 1 and 2 as above. Numbers 3 and 4 shall be drawn by lot; the first drawn shall be placed at the top of the second quarter; the second shall be placed at the bottom of the third quarter.

(c) If eight are to be seeded: Numbers 1, 2, 3 and 4 as above outlined. Numbers 5, 6, 7 and 8 shall be drawn by lot. The first name drawn shall be placed at the top of the second eighth (not already occupied by a seeded entrant) in the top half; the second name drawn shall be placed at the bottom of the third eighth (not already occupied by a seeded entrant) in the bottom half; the third name drawn shall be placed at the top of the fourth eighth (not already occupied by a seeded entrant) in the top half; and the fourth name drawn shall be placed at the bottom of the first eighth (not already occupied by a seeded entrant) in the bottom half.

(d) If sixteen are to be seeded: Numbers 1 to 8 shall be drawn as above outlined. Numbers 9 to

16 shall be drawn in similar manner except that they shall be drawn and placed in the upper half of the draw at the top of their respective sixteenths and in the lower half of the draw at the bottom of their respective sixteenths.

(e) Tournament Committees are advised for simplicity's sake to seed either two, four, eight or sixteen men (powers of 2) when possible, but if this is impracticable and an odd number is desired, the following method is prescribed:

(1) Two, four or sixteen entrants shall always be seeded as outlined above.

(2) If there are one, three, five or seven entrants to be seeded, determine by lot which half shall contain the larger number, i.e., 1, 2, 3, or 4; the other half therefore receiving 0, 1, 2, or 3. If there are two, four or six extra entrants to be seeded, half shall be seeded in the upper half of the draw and half in the lower.

(3) After this has been determined, the extra entrants shall be drawn by lot to determine which individual entrants shall go in each half; the first drawn to go in the upper half, the second drawn in the lower half, the third drawn in the upper half, and so on; the last drawn, in the case when the extra entrants are an odd number, to go into that half of the draw which by lot drew the greater number of players.

(4) After the extra entrants that are to be seeded in the two halves have been determined in the above manner, their position in the half varies according to the number of entrants that have previously been seeded, namely, two, four, or eight.

(5) Each extra entrant must be so placed as to

be in relatively the same position as all other seeded men. If there are more such positions than there are extra men to fill them, draw by lot which of these positions shall be occupied.

(6) If in making the draw for any USTA Championship or other tournaments sanctioned by USTA, the normal procedure operates to place in the same quarter domestic players having rank- ing of four or better from the same Sectional Association, or from the same school or family, or foreign players from the same country, the Com- mittee may, at its discretion place the second or later of such names drawn as nearly as possible in the same relative position in the next succeeding quarter not occupied by a domestic player having ranking of four or better from the same Sectional Association, or from the same school or family, or not occupied by a foreign player from the same country, as the case may be.

(7) After the places for the extra entrants have been ascertained they shall be filled from top to bottom by these entrants in the order in which they were drawn in Paragraph 2, Section (e) (3). In all cases the seeded entrants shall when possible be placed at the top of the quarters, eighths or six- teenths, as the case may be.

3. The names of all the remaining competitors shall be written on separate cards or papers, placed in a suitable receptacle, withdrawn one by one at random and copied on a sheet in the order drawn. The first name or names drawn shall constitute the byes (if any) not already filled by seeded men in the top half of the draw; the next name or names drawn shall constitute the places not al-

ready filled by seeded entrants in the first round; and the last name or names drawn shall constitute the byes (if any) not already filled by seeded entrants in the lower half of the draw.

4. The draw for handicap tournament shall be conducted in the following manner. The names of all competitors shall be written on separate cards or papers, placed in a suitable receptacle, withdrawn one by one at random and copied on a sheet in the order drawn. The first name or names drawn shall constitute the byes (if any) in the top half of the draw; the next name or names drawn shall constitute the first round: and the last name or names drawn shall constitute the byes (if any) in the lower half of the draw.

5. Foreign Entries. A Foreigner will not be considered as such for seeding purposes if he resides in this country and is ranked in the national or sectional rankings of the previous year.

(a) Foreign entrants of sufficient ability to warrant their being seeded shall be rated in order of ability and shall be drawn as provided in the foregoing paragraphs except that they shall be placed in the following positions: If there is but one foreign player to be seeded his name shall be placed at the bottom of the half of the draw not occupied by the number 1 domestic seed; if there are two such players number 1 shall be placed at the bottom of the half occupied by the number 2 domestic seed and the number 2 foreign seed shall be placed at the bottom of the other half.

(b) Numbers 3 and 4 of the Foreigners shall be drawn by lot and placed in the bottom of the quarters, not already occupied by Numbers 1 and

2 of the Foreigners. For eight or sixteen foreign players, proceed as in Paragraph 2, Section (c) or (d), but by placing them at the bottom of the eighths or sixteenths as the case may be. Except that if such procedure operates to place in the same quarter the seeded players of the same foreign nation the name drawn shall be placed at the bottom of the next succeeding eighth in a quarter not occupied by a National of the same foreign country and subsequent drawings shall be used successively to fill vacancies before proceeding in regular order.

(c) When seeding a number of Foreigners not a power of 2, proceed as in Paragraph 2, Section (e), except that the Foreigners shall, when possible, be placed at the bottom of the eighths or sixteenths, etc., as the case may be, and due regard shall be had for the exception in Paragraph 5, Section (b), which is designed to avoid the presence in the same quarter of the seeded players of the same foreign nation. In further pursuance of such objective, if more than four from the same nation are seeded, the fifth, sixth, etc. shall be so placed at the bottom of the quarters, eighths or sixteenths that each shall be separated from his own Nationals as widely as possible without displacing any names previously drawn. If, however, an odd number of Foreigners is drawn in the same draw with an odd number of Americans, the half receiving the greater number of Americans shall receive the smaller number of Foreigners, the other half therefore receiving one more Foreigner than Americans, but both sides receiving the same number of seeded players.

6. Infraction of the above rules renders a club or organization liable to loss of all tournaments for the following year; except that in competitions between nations, states, cities, clubs, colleges, schools and similar bodies, when the competition is really between such bodies and not between the players as individuals, the players may be placed in such manner as agreed upon by the management of the competition.

After the seeding is completed, draw and place other entrants as usual (see Regulation 21, Section 3).

Maximum number of sets. It is recommended that the maximum number of sets in all matches be 3, except that in USTA Men's singles and doubles championships, the maximum number of sets in all matches shall be 5.

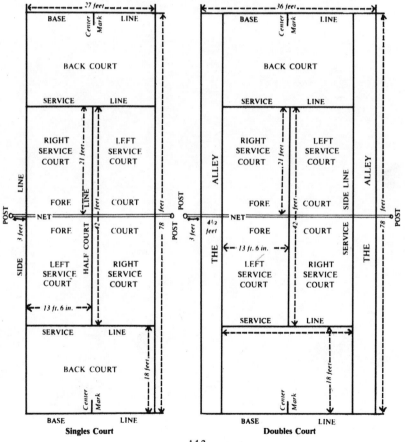

Diagram and Dimensions of Tennis Court

Singles Court

Doubles Court

113

Women's Lib and Professional Tennis *

by Harold Geist, Cecilia Martinez and Esme Emanuel

The Women's Liberation movement has reached far-flung fields, situations, and places never dreamed of by Susan B. Anthony or even Kate Millett. The movement has extended to professional tennis, spearheaded by the great Billie Jean King, who split off from the U.S. Lawn Tennis Association (U.S.L.T.A.), now the U.S. Tennis Association, to form a women's entourage. They have demanded equal pay in the tournaments with men and have boycotted the more prestigious tournaments.

In the sports area, no one has bothered to assess the psyche of the people who watch and pay to see the female gladiators. How do people really feel about female contestants competing along with the so-called superior male? At the U.S. National Tennis Tournament in Forest Hills, New York, in September 1970, Martinez and Emanuel, both participants in the tournament, took a survey on Sunday, September 7, of 94 women and 184 men who at-

---

*Reprinted from *Vocational Guidance Quarterly*, Sept. 1971. pp. 56–58.

tended the matches that day (see Figure 1). These spectators were selected at random in the general admission section of the stadium. This represented about 2 percent of the total turnout of the day.

We suppose that the best way to summarize the results of the questionnaire is that men answered (at least) that women should be equal to men in professional tennis, but the women spectators who answered thought the women tennis players should be more equal. The men enjoyed watching men's matches more than they did watching women's matches; by a slight margin (45 percent to 42 percent), the women enjoyed watching women about equally as men, and a very small percentage of both men and women spectators (9 percent and 13 percent, respectively) enjoyed watching women's matches more than men's.

Where the pocketbook is involved, a larger percentage of women (than men) would pay to watch tournaments with only women players, although the difference is not significant. More of the men spectators thought that men players should get twice as much money (this payment ratio being the most common) as the women. Not very surprising is that 50 percent of women spectators thought that women should get as much money as men.

A huge majority of these spectators wanted men and women to play in the same tournaments, perhaps because if the tournaments were separate, the spectators would have to pay double if they wanted to watch top men and women tennis players. The majority of both men and women spectators (42 percent and 53 percent, respectively) thought that just as many women should play as men, and the die-hard male woman-haters (burnt-child constellation?) and the equally die-hard female women-haters (insecure about their femininity?) were in an insignificant minority, since only 2 percent of men and 1 percent of women thought that there should be no women tennis players in the tournaments.

In answer to question 5, it seems that the majority of men come to watch women play tennis and not anything else, which may be a reflection on these men (some of the prettiest and most shapely women are in professional tennis —witness Helga Niessen Mastoff, Mary Eisel Curtis, and— modestly—Cecilia Martinez). However, a goodly number of women (71 percent) would come to watch only men play, which according to Freud is "healthy." Insofar as being in the limelight in tournaments is concerned (question 8) a larger percentage of women spectators thought that women should play as many matches as men on the grandstand and stadium courts.

Finally, the one question where there was almost unanimous opinion was the order of events in which the spectators preferred to watch tennis. Although men's singles were the first choice of both the men and women spectators, women's singles came ahead of men's doubles for both the men and women spectators. It may be that women are finally breaking free of the cultural constraints of an "enslaving" civilization. Even Freud would have approved of women tennis players freeing themselves from the subordination of domineering fathers.

FIGURE 1. *Tennis Questionnaire by Esme Emanuel and Cecilia Martinez*

The purpose of this questionnaire is to find certain trends of interest in tennis audiences.

Check one _____male _____female

		Men		Women		p
		N	%	N	%	Level
1)	Which do you enjoy watching more?					
	_____men's match	106	57	39	42	.05
	_____women's match	14	9	12	13	NS
	_____both equally well	64	34	43	45	NS
2)	Would you pay to watch a tournament with only women players?					
	_____yes	99	55	64	69	NS
	_____no	82	45	30	31	NS

3) Do you think the ratio of prize money
for men to women should be:

		Men		Women		p
		N	%	N	%	Level
_____1 to 1	(equal)	56	33	51	50	.01
_____2 to 1	(double)	63	36	28	27	.05
_____3 to 1	(triple)	34	19	11	11	NS
_____4 to 1		10	6	4	4	NS
_____5 to 1		10	6	8	8	NS

4) Do you think women players should:

	Men		Women		p
	N	%	N	%	Level
_____play their own tournaments separate from the men?	24	13	6	6	NS
_____play along with the men on the same tournaments?	151	82	87	92	.05
_____NOT play professional tennis?	7	5	1	2	NS

5) In a tournament with both men and
women players, do you think:

	Men				
_____women are just as interesting to watch as men?	89	54			
_____women are more interesting to watch than men?	19	11			
_____women are only an added attraction to the men?	60	35			

6) Do you think tournaments should include:

	Men		Women		p
_____as many women as men?	68	42	47	53	NS
_____three fourths as many women as men?	18	11	11	12	NS
_____half as many women as men?	50	30	15	17	.05
_____one fourth as many women as men?	9	6	5	6	NS
_____NO women?	3	2	1	1	NS
_____other (specify).	14	9	9	11	NS

7) If a tournament decided to eliminate
all the women's events, would you
pay to watch only the men play?

	Men		Women		p
_____yes	148	81	67	71	NS
_____no	35	19	27	29	NS

8) Do you think women should play as
many matches as men on the stadium
and grandstand courts?

	Men		Women		p
_____yes	97	56	63	71	.05
_____no	76	44	26	29	.05

9) Check the order of events in which you
prefer to watch tennis (number 1 to 5)

_____mixed doubles	5		4		
_____women's singles	2		2		
_____men's singles	1		1		
_____women's doubles	4		5		
_____men's doubles	3		3		

Glossary

AMERICAN TWIST SERVE—A serve hit by rotating the racket around the side and top of the ball causing the ball to bounce sharply both to the side and forward on the receiver's court.

CANNONBALL SERVE—A very hard serve.

CHIP SHOT—A shot hit farther than a drop shot but not as far as a full drive. Usually a chip shot is sliced or chopped.

CHOP—A ball that is hit full force but is sliced or cut; there is a spin on the ball.

DINK—A return of serve hit just over the net, usually farther than a drop shot but not as far as a regular return.

DOUBLES SENSE—The ability to play as a team, coordinate as partners, and back each other up.

DROP SHOT—A shot that lands close to the net on the opponent's side.

FAKE OUT—To deceive one's opponent by looking one way and hitting another or by positioning one's body as if to hit one kind of shot and hitting another.

FLAT DRIVE—A ball hit full force with the racket flat against the ball.

FLAT SERVE—A serve hit with the racket flat or flush against the ball so that there will be no spin on the ball either in the air or when it bounces on the other side of the net.

FLUB—A bad error; a "miss" especially on a set-up or easy shot.

GAMESMANSHIP—The use of behavior designed to aggravate or throw off one's opponent to one's own advantage.

GROOVED—(Strokes) smooth and perfectly timed.

KEEPING OPPONENT "HONEST"—Hitting occasional shots down the net man's alley to prevent his poaching too often.

LOB—A stroke in which the ball is hit high in the air, often toward the back court to the opponent's side of the court.

LOB VOLLEY—A stroke in which a lob is hit off a volley (see Lob, Volley).

NO-ADD GAME—Instead of 15, 30, 40, deuce and add in scoring, it is 1, 2, 3, and no-add. At 3-all in points, the receiver chooses the side he wants to return the ball in, and whoever wins the point wins the game.

NO MAN'S LAND—The area around the service line, where the player sometimes is caught having to pick up and return a ball at his feet, especially when coming in behind a serve.

OVERHEAD—A shot that one must make by stroking above his head; a stroke made over one's head.

PASSING SHOT—A shot that goes beyond where the opponent is positioned, hit on either side of him.

PERCENTAGE TENNIS—Tennis played conservatively and safely, taking into account the odds by not making risky shots.

POACH—In doubles, to invade one's partner's territory.

PRESS—To hit forcing shots especially deep and hard attempting to force the opponent into error.

PSYCH OUT—To dominate one's opponent psychologically.

PSYCH UP—To toughen or build oneself mentally in preparation for a match.

PUSH—To play safe, soft-balling to keep the ball in the court.

PUT-AWAY SHOT—A clean winner; a shot the opponent cannot return.

SEED—To rank (players) according to their tennis records and ability.

SET-UP—An easy shot to put away; an easy shot with which to win a point.

SEVERE TOPSPIN—A return of serve in which the racket comes across the top of the ball as it is hit, causing it to bounce sharply in the direction in which it is hit.

SLICE—A return in which the receiver "cuts" the ball by either hitting under it or hitting on the side of it.

SLICE KICK SERVE—A serve that has a "cut" on it, causing it not only to bounce sideways on landing, but also to "kick off," or have an extra propulsive movement.

SLICE SERVE—A serve in which the racket is rotated around the ball, causing it to bounce to one side on landing.

SOFT VOLLEY—A volley in which the ball is hit over the net with very little speed.

STOP VOLLEY—A volley hit just over the net, like a drop shot; the ball dies when it hits the playing surface.

TELEGRAPH—To let one's opponent know where one intends to hit the ball by footwork, body position, and racket handling.

TOPSPIN—Forward rotation of the ball, causing it to drop quickly after reaching the peak of its trajectory and to move faster on the rebound.

TOPSPIN LOB—A lob hit with topspin (see Lob, Topspin).

UNDERCUT—To hit the ball by sliding the racket underneath the ball. This is sometimes done when serving to disconcert the opponent.

UNGROOVE—To change rhythm or timing.

VOLLEY—A stroke in which one hits the ball before it bounces.

Index

123